.50

Tax Impacts
on Compensation

Daniel M. Holland

Dan Throop Smith

Alvin M. David

Curtis R. Henderson

Kenneth C. Foster

Lloyd E. Slater

V. Henry Rothschild, 2nd

Wilbur G. Lewellen

Christopher Branda, Jr.

U. E. Landauer

Thomas R. Donahue

John R. Lindquist

Dan M. McGill

William T. Gibb, III

Leonard Lesser

Russell H. Hubbard

Laurence N. Woodworth

Symposium conducted by the

TAX INSTITUTE OF AMERICA

October 3-4, 1968

Princeton
TAX INSTITUTE OF AMERICA
1969

A TAX INSTITUTE OF AMERICA PUBLICATION

The purpose of the annual symposium conducted by the Tax Institute of America [formerly Tax Institute Incorporated] is to focus attention on a major problem of taxation by affording an opportunity for discussion by informed participants representing different points of view. The publication of this volume carries with it, of course, no endorsement of the views—sometimes conflicting—of the various participants.

Library of Congress Catalog Card Number: 70-90256

SYMPOSIUM COMMITTEES

PROGRAM COMMITTEE

Chairman: HERMAN C. BIEGEL, Attorney, Lee, Toomey & Kent

GEORGE S. ALLAN, Tax Counsel, Ford Motor Company

ROBERT E. ROYES, Secretary, Employees Benefit Committee, American Telephone and Telegraph Company

DAN THROOP SMITH, Professor of Finance, Harvard Graduate School of Business Administration

ROY A. WENTZ, JR., Chief Counsel, Federal and Foreign Tax Division, E. I. du Pont de Nemours & Company

Ex Officio:

F. CLEVELAND HEDRICK, JR., Attorney, Hedrick and Lane, and President, Tax Institute of America

MABEL WALKER, Executive Director, Tax Institute of America

COMMITTEE OF HOSTS

Chairman: HUGH M. MCNEILL, Assistant Comptroller, Continental Can Company, Inc.

C. A. BURLESON, Director of Taxes, General Telephone & Electronics Corporation

ROBERT J. CASEY, Attorney, Clark, Carr & Ellis

MURRAY DRABKIN, Attorney, New York

C. LOWELL HARRISS, Professor of Economics, Columbia University; Economic Consultant, Tax Foundation, Inc.

CHARLES L. KADES, Attorney, Hawkins, Delafield & Wood

T. M. KUPFER, CPA, Haskins & Sells

ERNEST KURNOW, Professor of Statistics, Schools of Business, New York University

JANET K. MESSING, Associate Professor of Economics, Herbert H. Lehman College of the City University of New York

SYMPOSIUM FUND COMMITTEE

Chairman: D. H. LARMEE, Vice President—Taxes and Financial Administration, Pullman Incorporated

VICTOR E. FERRALL, General Tax Attorney, American Telephone and Telegraph Company

F. W. STANDEFER, Director—Taxes, Gulf Oil Corporation

FOREWORD

THE LATE Justice Cardoza stated more than 35 years ago that: "One can read in the revisions of the Revenue Acts the record of the government's endeavor to keep pace with the fertility of invention whereby taxpayers contrive to keep the larger benefits of ownership and be relieved of the attendant burdens." (*Burnet* v. *Wells*, 289 U.S. 670, 675 [1933]). Perhaps in no other field of the law is this more dramatically evidenced than with respect to the impact of taxes on methods and levels of compensation—the subject matter of the 1968 Symposium of the Tax Institute of America.

In the early 1940's a highly precise and articulated statutory scheme was adopted relating to qualified pension and profit-sharing plans. This was done so as to require a broad base for tax qualifications and to blunt the efforts of ingenious consultants to set up pension plans for a handful of highly compensated officers and stockholders.

Then came the 50's, with the almost indiscriminate use of qualified stock options, split dollar insurance plans, and similar devices. The stock option device was considerably circumscribed by subsequent legislation. The effectiveness of the split dollar insurance plan was substantially curtailed by reconsideration at the Administrative level.

Now in the 60's, the Treasury and the Congress have had second thoughts about the applicable scope of the present provisions dealing with qualified pension and profit-sharing plans. The President's Cabinet Committee Report, issued in January, 1965, suggested whole areas for reconsideration. The Administration's bill, introduced by Senator Ralph Yarborough and Congressman John H. Dent in the respective Houses, would require an even

v

more radical series of guidelines for qualified pension and profit-sharing plans.

All of this indicates the immediacy of the symposium program on "Impact of Taxes on Methods and Levels of Compensation," conducted by the Tax Institute of America. Economic aspects of the tax impacts were analyzed by distinguished economists. Eminent authorities discussed how taxes affect benefit plans for employees generally. This discussion brought into focus the development of plans under the existing statute for the benefit of employes as a whole.

At another session, equally distinguished speakers considered how taxes affect benefit plans for executives, and discussed the various incentive compensation devices currently in vogue that are designed to provide executives with additional compensation in the most salutary tax form.

On the second day of the symposium there was discussion of conceptual problems in the President's Cabinet Committee Report on existing pension legislation. The necessity for the new guidelines was explored by persons who have had in the past several years an important role in the development of, and the opposition to, those concepts. Finally, the closing speaker outlined current legislative developments.

The symposium was especially fortunate this year in two respects. The quality of the papers presented was at an extremely high level. Moreover, the comments of the panelists, as well as the enthusiastic participation by the audience, made the sessions rewarding and provocative.

In order to expedite publication, the Institute engaged Miss Geneva Seybold as special editor for the volume. We are indebted to her for careful editing of the symposium material.

HERMAN C. BIEGEL
Attorney, Lee, Toomey & Kent, and
Chairman, Symposium Program Committee

CONTENTS

vii

PART ONE

ECONOMIC ASPECTS OF TAXES ON COMPENSATION

CHAPTER I

PENSION FUND GROWTH AND ITS ECONOMIC IMPLICATIONS*

DANIEL M. HOLLAND

Professor of Finance, Alfred P. Sloan School of Management, Massachusetts Institute of Technology

PENSION funds are collections of financial assets—cash, bonds of governments or business firms, stock, mortgages and the like—accumulated in recognition of the obligations for retirement and related payments incurred by pension plans. Because pension funds are set up in connection with pension plans, our discussion of pension fund growth and its consequences starts with the growth of pension plans. In particular, we shall be interested in those plans whose funds are geared to the actuarial value of the promises made under the plans or some reasonable facsimile thereof.

A HISTORY OF GROWTH

Not all plans run funds of this kind. Sovereign governments can, if necessary, always meet benefit payments promised under their pension programs, through the use of the taxing power or exercise of their monopoly of the right to print money. While it is fairly common practice, therefore, to have some sort of fund associated with social security programs of national governments, such as OASDI in the United States, it is very uncommon for the

---

* I wish to acknowledge at the outset my great indebtedness to two men who were colleagues on a study of the economic effect of pensions undertaken by the National Bureau of Economic Research—Roger Murray, who directed the project, and Phillip Cagan. In later sections of this paper I draw heavily on their work and cite it frequently. But this falls far short of indicating how much I have learned from them.

3

accumulated assets to be at all close to the present value of the benefit payments obligated under the plan. Thus, for example, between 1955 and 1965, the actuarial value of OASDI's benefit promises increased enormously while its fund fell slightly from $21.7 billion to $19.8 billion.

All business firms, however, are potentially mortal and lack taxing and money-printing powers. Consequently it is considered good practice for a company to "back up" its pension with a corpus of assets separate from those used in its industrial operations. While the assets of the fund are related to the present value of expected benefit payments under the plan, at no point in time is there a one-to-one correspondence between the two. Nevertheless, while fund dynamics have a pattern of their own, an increase in the scope or size of a pension plan's promises in a given year will be reflected primarily in increased fund accumulations in the years following.

State and local governments, too, in connection with the pension plans they provide for their own employees, characteristically set up funds. Our review of pension plan and fund growth deals with the pension plans and associated funds set up both by private businesses and by state and local governments for their employees. Our discussion of economic effects will concentrate on private industrial plans because, in some aspects, they have received closer study; because, on a number of points, they pose more pressing problems; and because in order of magnitude business and industrial plans are currently considerably higher. Many of the conclusions relating to private industrial plans, however, are extendible directly or with modification to state and local government plans.

The two groups of pension plans—those set up by business firms and those established by state and local governments—have a long history, but in the last quarter of a century they have been characterized by extremely rapid rates of growth. They have developed into major sources of income security, on the one hand, and prominent financial intermediaries, on the other. Assertions about rapid growth are borne out by the indicia in Table 1, for private industrial plans, and in Table 2, for state-local government plans. While the tables tell their own story, a few highlights can be noted.

4

The number of workers covered by private industrial plans is now over six times as great as the number 25 years ago and, more pointedly, the percentage of employees in nonagricultural industry (excluding government workers who are covered by their own plans) has risen from under 15 per cent to over 50 per cent.[1]

Coincident with the growth of coverage, of course, has been a huge expansion of the fiscal operations of industrial pension plans. Thus:

1. Contributions in 1965 ran at more than 25 times their 1940 level.

2. Beneficiaries in 1965 were nearly 15 times the number in 1940, and benefit payments amounted to more than 30 times the payments in 1940.

3. With contributions exceeding benefit payments, assets have been accumulating in the funds. Indeed, by 1965 the funds themselves had increased to almost 36 times their 1940 level in book value terms (considerably more, were their market value used as basis for comparison). As funds increase in size, more earnings will eventuate: they have, by rough estimate, increased by a factor of 18 times. Finally, in terms of funds "squirreled away," (the net investment each year, which is the result of the excess of the fund inflows of contributions and earnings over the outflows of benefit payments), private industrial pension funds accumulated during the year 1965 over 20 times as much in the way of financial assets as in 1940. This latter figure, which measures the strength the funds bring to bear in the capital markets, (i.e., their importance as a source of funds for capital formation), rates particular attention because it is associated with two critically important economic activities—savings and investment.

Much the same story can be told for state and local pension funds. The plans for employees of state and local governments

[1] Even 50 per cent, however, in a very real sense, is an understatement of the current degree of coverage. For part-time workers are not as "suitable" for pensions, either in terms of an employer's obligations or the ease with which appropriate arrangements can be developed for them. Neither are young workers who may try a number of jobs and employers before they "settle in." Defining young to be under 25 and removing them and voluntary part-time workers from the total that we might expect pensions to be provided for would, of course, leave a smaller base that would show a considerably higher coverage percentage for those who might reasonably be expected to be covered. See Daniel M. Holland, *Private Pension Funds: Projected Growth*, New York, National Bureau of Economic Research, 1966, p. 21.

TABLE 1

GROWTH OF PRIVATE INDUSTRIAL PENSION AND DEFERRED PROFIT
SHARING PLANS IN THE UNITED STATES, 1940-1965

	1940	1945	1950	1955	1960	1965
Coverage (millions of persons)	4.1	6.4	9.8	15.4	21.2	25.4
Employees in all industries except government and agriculture (millions of persons)	28.2	34.5	39.2	43.8	45.8	50.7
Percentage covered (per cent)	14.5	18.6	25.0	35.2	46.3	50.1
Contributions (billions of dollars)	0.3	1.0	2.1	3.8	5.5	7.8
Beneficiaries (millions of persons)	0.2	0.3	0.5	1.0	1.8	2.8
Benefit payments (billions of dollars)	0.1	0.2	0.4	0.8	1.8	3.2
Earnings[1] (billions of dollars)	0.2	0.3	0.5	0.7	1.7	3.6
Assets (billions of dollars)	2.4	5.4	12.1	27.5	52.0	85.4
Increase in assets[2] (billions of dollars)	0.4	1.1	2.2	3.7	5.4	8.2

[1] Calculated as residual from rounded numbers, hence subject to relatively substantial error.
[2] In the given year. Figures for 1940-1950 are rough estimates.

Sources: Raymond W. Goldsmith, A Study of Savings in the United States, Princeton, Princeton University Press, 1955-56; Walter W. Kolodrubetz, "Employee Benefit Plans in 1966," Social Security Bulletin, 31 (April, 1968); U.S. Department of Labor, Bureau of Labor Statistics, Handbook of Labor Statistics, 1967, (BLS Bulletin No. 1555).

have great accumulative potential that has not yet been properly appreciated.[2]

What we have witnessed over the last quarter century has been the development of a private pension structure of imposing magnitude. Incidentally, subject to particular national modifications, such has also been the case in the other major industrialized countries of North America and Western Europe. Accounting for this development are a number of factors that range from broad sociological-economic changes and demographic factors to particular income tax encouragements and advantages.

In the United States, taxes have been an encouraging factor, and have also affected the timing of the acceleration of pension plan growth. While private industrial pension plans can be found

[2] This is discussed in Roger F. Murray, Economic Aspects of Pensions: A Summary Report, New York, National Bureau of Economic Research, 1968, 132 p., and in Holland, op. cit. supra note 1.

TABLE 2

GROWTH OF STATE AND LOCAL GOVERNMENT EMPLOYEE PENSION PLANS AND FUNDS IN THE UNITED STATES, 1940-1965

	1940	1945	1950	1955	1960	1965
Coverage (millions of persons) Employees of state and local government	1.4	1.8	2.6	3.5	4.5	5.8
(millions of persons) Percentage covered	3.3	3.2	4.3	5.1	6.4	8.0
(per cent) Contributions	42.4	56.3	60.5	68.8	70.3	72.5
(billions of dollars) Beneficiaries	0.3	0.4	0.9	1.7	2.9	4.2
(millions of persons) Benefit payments	0.2	0.2	0.3	0.4	0.7	0.9
(billions of dollars) Earnings[1]	0.1	0.2	0.3	0.6	1.0	1.7
(billions of dollars) Assets	—	—	—	—	0.4	0.9
(billions of dollars) Increase in assets[2]	1.6	2.5	5.2	10.6	19.7	33.6
(billions of dollars)	—	—	—	—	2.3	3.4

[1] Calculated as a residual from rounded numbers, hence subject to relatively substantial error.
[2] In the given year.

Sources: Institute of Life Insurance, *Private and Public Pension Plans in the United States,* New York (second edition, 1967) pp. 16-17; U.S. Department of Labor, Bureau of Labor Statistics, *Handbook of Labor Statistics, 1967* (BLS Bulletin No. 1555), p. 69.

at least as far back as 1875, tax and regulatory actions during World War II provided a powerful fillip to their growth. The introduction of high and sharply progressive rates of personal income tax made compensation arrangements in which tax payments could be deferred more attractive. For they provided a way for injecting some long-run averaging in the taxation of the income stream and, for the usual case, a lower lifetime tax liability. During the war, more particularly, interest by unions in pensions was enhanced, because the stabilization policy limited directed wage increases. For the same reason employers utilized pension arrangements to a greater extent to attract or hold scarce workers. Quite likely, although perhaps not rationally, the high corporate rates levied at that time made pensions seem relatively "costless," and so hastened their adoption or extension to more workers,[3] as

---

[3] "Perhaps not rationally" because wage increases would also be a deductible business expense, and high wartime rates might well not be expected to prevail in peacetime.

7

did the provision of the Internal Revenue Code of 1942 requiring that for a pension plan to be nondiscriminatory (and hence have the employer's contribution to it free of corporate tax) it must not be directed narrowly to top officers or selected small groups of employees.

Further impetus to the spread of pension programs came from the inclusion of a pension as part of the coal strike settlement in 1946, from the decision by the National Labor Relations Board in the Inland Steel Case in 1948 (upheld by the Supreme Court in 1949) that pensions are a bargainable issue, and from the Steel Industry Fact Finding Board's recommendation of a pension program, in 1949.

The growth of pension programs is also a response to deeper underlying needs and changes in the country's structure and economy. An important demographic basis for the growth in pension programs has been the steady and substantial increase in the older population. Between 1900 and 1965, those 65 and over increased almost six-fold, from 3.1 million to 18.2 million, a rate of increase considerably greater than that for the total population. Thus persons 65 and over represented 4.1 per cent of the population in 1900, and 9.3 per cent by 1965.[4]

These figures reflect increasing life expectancy, but an even stronger thrust for pensions comes from the steady decrease in the number of years those who survive to, say, 60, can be expected to spend in employment.[5] So while there has been a rather mild increase in life expectancies, there has been a sharp increase in the years of nonworking old age.[6] The movement of population from

---

[4] For the 1900 data see U.S. Bureau of the Census, *Historical Statistics of the United States,* statistical abstract supplement prepared with the cooperation of the Social Science Research Council, Washington, p. 7; for the 1965 data see U.S. Bureau of the Census, *Statistical Abstract of the United States, 1966,* Washington, p. 6.

[5] This trend predates the rapid growth of pensions, but could very well have been accelerated by their development. To some extent there is a "chicken-egg" argument here.

[6] In 1900, a white male at age 60 had a life expectancy of 14.3 years, of which 11.5 years would be spent in the labor force and 2.8 in retirement. His counterpart in 1940 had only a slightly increased life expectancy—15.1 years—but expected time in the labor force had declined to 9.2 years and expected retirement had increased to 5.9 years. This sharp change in the years of nonworking old age predates the ground swell of pensions.

A more recent estimate shows not much change since 1940, for similar data (al-the countryside to the city and from agriculture to manufacturing and service trades also pushes in the direction of the replacement of informal family-oriented income support in old age to more formal work-oriented arrangements.

The growth of pensions, then, appears to be a response to underlying structural changes in the economy as well as to particular tax advantages. And this growth also suggests that income support in old age may be a "commodity" with an income elasticity greater than one, i.e., that as income expands, the portion of it devoted to providing for old age increases more than proportionately. This seems so far to have taken a variety of forms: more generous benefits for a given retirement age, a wider variety of options under retirement plans, earlier retirement ages, etc.

Perhaps it is no coincidence that what we have witnessed in the last 25 years or so has been a change in the way workers prefer to receive their productivity gains. Traditionally they have taken the form of some increase in real income and some decline in hours worked. Since 1940, with the exception of the war years, average weekly hours worked by production workers in manufacturing have, if anything, risen somewhat, but in prior years there was a tendency for the average work week to decline.[7] It was this observation that led to Roger Murray's suggestive conclusion that "employee preferences have shifted to some extent, from the desire for more leisure during their working years to a greater degree of financial independence during retirement or to earlier retirement."[8]

---

though not strictly comparable, since the data of 1960 refer to all male workers) indicate that a male worker who survived to 60 could expect to live 15.8 more years, of which 8.5 would be in the labor force and 7.3 in retirement. (The data for 1900 and 1940 are from U.S. Department of Labor, Bureau of Labor Statistics, *Tables of Working Life; Length of Working Life for Men*, BLS Bulletin No. 1001, Washington, 1950, p. 42. The 1960 figure is from Stuart Garfinkle, "Table of Working Life for Men, 1960," *Monthly Labor Review*, 86 (July, 1963), 822.)

[7] In 1940 the average of weekly hours worked by production workers in manufacturing was 38.1, in 1950 it was 40.5, and in 1965 it was 41.2. Similar but not strictly comparable data show a decline from 51.0 in 1909 to 38.1 by 1940.

[8] Murray, *op. cit. supra* note 2, p. 5. Murray notes, however, that vacations and paid holidays did increase over the period during which average hours worked remained ostensibly unchanged (or even increased slightly). So the point is not unambiguous.

Projected Growth

The quick review of the record of the past revealed high rates of growth and impressive magnitudes associated with coverage, beneficiaries, and related fiscal activities of pension plans. As we look ahead, rates of growth can be expected to tail off simply as a natural consequence of absolute magnitudes becoming large. Moreover, it is to be expected that coverage will increase more slowly than in the past, since the more difficult areas—smaller firms, transient employment situations, etc.—are the ones that will have to be tapped. In terms of pure size, however, pension funds and associated fiscal operations are likely over the next 15 years to reach levels that dwarf the present magnitudes. This is due in large part to the basic dynamics of pension fund accumulation which permit some pretty fair guesses about the future from what has already happened. Another reason for expecting further very substantial growth in pension funds is the fact that plans characteristically have undergone considerable "improvement" in the size of their benefits and associated protection; such improvements, with a lag, are mirrored in the size of funds.

What might be expected as the future path of the private industrial pension plan structure (and the plans for state-local government employees as well) can be developed by analogy with the typical pension plan. Suppose, for a start, that the numbers and age and sex composition of the firm's working force is constant, then we could expect the dynamics of its pension fund accumulation to run something like this: Initially, with contributions geared to the level of future benefit payments and current benefits running at very low levels, there is a rapid accumulation of assets in the fund. As the fund's accumulated earnings become larger, and as more workers retire, benefits grow relative to contributions. At some point, indeed, benefit payments will exceed contributions, but for a while accumulation will still take place, because earnings on the larger fund will more than make up the difference. Eventually, however, with a pension plan population fixed, as assumed above, there will come a time when benefits will just equal the sum of earnings and contributions. The plan, then, will have matured, and its fund will no longer grow. By definition, however, the plan of a growing firm will never mature, since more workers will enter employment, wage scales will rise, benefit formulas will be liberalized, and other options will typically be offered under the plan. There is a strong possibility that eventually the annual amount of fund accumulation will drop, i.e., the annual first differences of the aggregate of pension fund assets will be successively smaller, although their reaching zero (or closely approaching it) is not a very real possibility in a growing economy.

The schematics of the time path do not, of course, tell us anything about the duration of the process. We know, however, from the foregoing artificial example, that the process has a long time span. In the contrived situation of unchanging ratios among all the relevant variables, if a firm's work force averaged 40 years of age, and the retirement age were set at 65, the pension plan would "mature" after 25 years. In real life, and for the aggregate of plans, what is likely to happen? I have made some projections which give an answer—partial and imperfect at best—over the next decade or so. The projections, it turns out, with the 20-20 hindsight that only the passage of time can give, partake of the nature of so much that we have to work with in life—they are not correct, but they are useful. They are set forth for private industrial plans

TABLE 3

PROJECTIONS OF PRIVATE INDUSTRIAL AND STATE-LOCAL
EMPLOYEES PENSION FUNDS, SELECTED YEARS, 1965-1980

	1965[a]	1970	1975	1980
Private Industrial Plans				
Coverage (millions of persons)	25.4	32.6	37.2	41.4
Beneficiaries (millions of persons)	2.8	4.1	6.0	8.0
Benefit payments (billions of dollars)	3.2	4.7	7.3	10.6
Fund assets (billions of dollars)	85.4	116.9	155.2	193.1
Annual change in fund assets (billions of dollars)	8.2	7.5	7.6	7.4
State-Local Government Employee Plans				
Coverage (millions of persons)	5.8	7.6	9.6	12.2
Beneficiaries (millions of persons)	0.9	0.9	1.1	1.3
Benefit payments (billions of dollars)	1.8	2.0	2.6	3.4
Fund assets (billions of dollars)	33.6	50.7	76.9	114.9
Annual change in fund assets (billions of dollars)	3.4	4.2	6.0	8.9

a Actual values. (See Tables 1 and 2).
    Source: Daniel M. Holland, *Private Pension Funds: Projected Growth,* New York, National Bureau of Economic Research, 1966; state-local fund data converted to calendar year basis.

and state-local plans in Table 3. These and other sets of projections appear in my book, *Private Pension Funds: Projected Growth,* that was published by the National Bureau of Economic Research in 1966.

From the estimates in Table 3, some of the stages in the fiscal dynamics of pension plans can be distinguished. Thus, while coverage of industrial plans will continue to grow in the next 15 years, in all likelihood it will be at a slower pace than in the past. On the other hand, the number of beneficiaries and amount of benefit payments to them will both pick up steam. Yet earnings, not explicitly tabulated, will grow rapidly enough to keep the corpus of pension fund assets increasing substantially. The estimate for 1980 is more than double the fund level at the end of 1965. And there is reason to believe that my projections have a downward bias, so the level of fund assets achieved by the end of 1980 could be noticeably larger than the projected value.[9] Be that as it may, there are signs of a peaking in the annual amount of fund accumulations and a suggestion, therefore, that fund growth may "slow down" by 1980. (This condition of constancy or even decline in the annual first differences of fund levels is a far cry from "maturity," which would be characterized by no change in fund levels from year to year.) The pattern traced by these projections suggests that industrial pension funds right now are having at least as powerful an effect on the annual flow of savings and in their bearing on the capital markets (at least as a source of funds) as they are likely to in the future.

Not so, however, for funds of plans for state-local government employees. Here the projections portend a different prospect. Buoyed by the projected high rate of growth of employment in the government sector as compared with manufacturing and service trades, coverage and contributions will continue to grow rapidly. And reflecting the relatively recent entry into employment of most workers in this area, beneficiaries and payments to them will move up more modestly than for industrial plans. Conse-

---

[9] This suspicion comes from a shortfall in the several most recent years between my projections (made at an earlier date) and the level of funds' assets as actually measured.

quently, annual fund accumulations will still show absolute growth from year to year, and fund levels will be considerably higher in 15 years; the 1980 total of accumulated assets will be 3.4 times the 1965 level (as contrasted with the projected ratio of 2.3 for private industrial plans.) Thus the projections indicate that up through 1980, the pension funds for state-local employee plans will continue to play a more important role each year in the process of saving and the markets for capital. Indeed, in 15 years they may very well be a more important source of funds than private industrial plans.

So much for the numbers, both as regards the history of growth to date and the possibilities for the future. But what of their significance? What difference does it make? This, after all, is our real interest.

Economic Effects—Saving

By a homely analogy, the fiscal operations of pension plans can be likened to a bathtub with the faucets running, i.e., contributions plus fund earnings, and the drain open, i.e., benefit payments. In the past, the rate of outflow through the drain has been less rapid than the force of the flow through the faucet, and our projections suggest that this will continue. So every year, the level of water in the tub is higher than in the year before. We call this difference, variously, pension fund accumulation, saving via pension funds, or pension fund investment. As economists view these terms, particularly the latter two—saving and investment—this puts pension funds at the very heart of two crucially important economic activities. For both savings and investment are processes intimately related to the primary goals of every economy, viz., growth and stability.

We define saving to be that portion of total output that is not currently consumed. In effect, then, it is the seed-corn of our economy which, if properly taken up by investment opportunities, would cause economic activity in the future to be more productive than it has been in the past. This is the role that saving plays in economic growth. The process is not automatic, since the savings plans of the community may fall short of (or exceed) the investment opportunities that entrepreneurs desire to implement.

So economic stability, too, is involved via the matching or mis-matching of savings desires and investment plans. Since saving enables capital formation but does not ensure it, what happens as regards capital formation and the markets through which capital is allocated is, in a sense, the other side of the coin. The annual change in pension fund assets—in popular parlance, their saving and/or investment—is large, and seemingly an important con-tributor to the total annual flow.

To turn to saving first, from Table 4 it would appear that a goodly fraction of total personal saving, 40 per cent in 1965 for example, can be attributed to retirement saving—defined in this connection to be the annual increase in private industrial and

TABLE 4

PAST AND PROJECTED RETIREMENT SAVING AND
RELATED VARIABLES FOR SELECTED PERIODS: 1946-1975

	Average 1946-50	Average 1951-55	Average 1956-60	Average 1961-65	1965	1975
Personal income (billions of dollars)	203.0	283.4	366.0	472.0	537.8	894.9
Personal saving (billions of dollars)	11.7	17.2	19.9	23.2	27.2	48.5
Retirement saving (billions of dollars)	2.7	4.6	7.2	9.9	10.9	15.1
Personal saving as per-centage of personal income (per cent)	5.8	6.1	5.4	4.9	5.1	5.4
Retirement saving as percentage of personal income (per cent)	1.3	1.6	2.0	2.1	2.0	1.7
Retirement saving as percentage of personal saving (per cent)	23.1	26.7	36.2	42.7	40.1	31.1

Source: Roger F. Murray, *Economic Aspects of Pensions: A Summary Report*, New York, National Bureau of Economic Research, 1968, pp. 54 and 62.

state-local pension plan assets.[10] This could mean that pension funds could be playing a major role in an important economic process. Or it could merely be a triumph of semantics. For simply to call something saving does not establish that in fact it is saving in the sense in which we have been using the term. Specifically,

---

[10] The data of Table 4, derived in part from different sources, and those of Tables 1, 2, and 3, are not completely consistent. Thus, in Table 4 retirement saving as defined above comes to $10.9 billion, while the sum of the annual changes in assets for the two categories of funds is $11.6 billion. Discrepancies of this size are in-consequential relative to the uses to which the data are put here.

simply to assert that pension funds "save" $10,9 billion a year does not establish that, because of this activity of theirs, an additional $10.9 billion that would not otherwise have been forthcoming is available for capital formation. For it could be that compensating offsets to pension fund "saving" occur. That is why it is crucially important to ask "What difference does it make that provision of income for retirement is made via pension plans which accumulate funds that bear some close correspondence to the actuarial value of the plans' pension obligations?" A change has occurred in the way income-maintenance in retirement is arranged for. As with any change in the way something is done in our economy, we should seek to find out whether these net annual accumulations represent net new savings or are simply a change in the form in which savings are made.

The significance can be pursued on both an analytical and empirical level and, thanks to the recent work of Phillip Cagan and George Katona, with the possibility of a less ambiguous answer than characterizes many such real-life economic questions. We proceed first with how the question might have been analyzed prior to their work.[11]

On an a priori basis we could approach the problem via what we would expect as regards the relative effect of a decline in price of one member of a set of closely substitutable commodities on the sales of that particular commodity compared with sales of the whole class of commodities in which it falls. Specifically, if the price of Scotch whisky were cut substantially, but other high-proof beverages remained unchanged in price, a safe prediction is that people would buy more Scotch, and we would expect total consumption of spirituous liquors to go up. To all but the most addicted drinker of Scotch, however, other whiskies are to some degree a substitute for it. Therefore, we would also expect, in the aggregate, purchases of Irish whisky, bourbon, Canadian whisky, etc., to fall, because Scotch is being substituted for them in con-

---

[11] Cagan and Katona are emphasized because of the substantial empirical work that buttresses their conclusion. It should be noted, however, that George Garvy at an earlier date recognized the possibility of the effect they discovered. George Garvy, "The Effect of Private Pension Plans on Personal Savings," *Review of Economics and Statistics*, August, 1950, 223-226. This was pointed out by Murray, *op. cit. supra* note 2.

sumption. Taking consumers' preference as given, the consumption of other commodities in the same class will fall, and thus, while the consumption of spirituous liquors as a class will have increased, that increase will not be as large as the expanded consumption of Scotch alone.

So, too, we might argue as regards pension saving. Something like a decline in price relative to other kinds of saving exists for this form because of the employers' support of it and the postponement of income tax on contributions made by the employer to the fund and on the fund's earnings. So pension saving should go up, which it has, but savings in other forms, i.e., made via other arrangements, insofar as they could serve some of the purposes that pension savings are made for, may be expected to decline. On net balance, then, total saving will rise, but not by as much as the increase in pension fund saving per se. All this, I repeat, is where we would come by pure deduction. While the argument seems to say something about the nature of the effect, it has nothing to say about its magnitude. That would depend importantly on the degree of substitutability between pension fund accumulation and other forms of saving.

However, even in this theoretical argument, there should be, in the back of our minds some place, a consideration which is all too frequently dismissed by the assumptions laid out at the start of the chain of reasoning, to the effect that people's preferences are taken as given. For, to revert to Scotch, it could be that people who had never before tried it would buy a bottle or two when its price had been cut, would learn to like it very much, and would consume more Scotch and not cut their consumption of other whiskies much, if at all. This would be a "learning" or "recognition"[12] effect which involves a change in people's preferences. The change in price has led to a learning experience in consumption which has caused a shift in the demand schedule. So, too, with pensions. Upon the institution of formal pension plans, people may "recognize" that they now have an expectation of some modicum of income support in old age, and this may induce them to save even

---

[12] The phrase "recognition effect" and a good deal of the discussion that follows are due to Professor Phillip Cagan. (See reference to his book in note 16.)

more, to convert that modicum to something more substantial. So the aggregate of savings, via pension and all other forms as well, might rise. This is a possibility that should not really be too surprising. For example, I think it is generally accepted in the trade that a good prospect for insurance is the man who has "learned" about it (acquired a taste for it) for the first time via the basic modicum provided by G.I. insurance.

Reverting to the possibility of substitution, there is also some empirical evidence that seems to support the expectation that pension fund savings will not be net new additions to the flow of personal saving, but rather will be made at the expense of alternative forms of saving. Over half a century—from 1897 through 1949—Raymond Goldsmith in his study of saving in the American economy discovered that the ratio of personal saving (including consumer durables) to personal income appears to have been substantially constant. Constancy, too, has characterized the proportions of total savings made by the personal, corporate, and government sectors respectively (if saving through social security and other governmental trust funds is included in personal savings).[13]

This outcome over a long period of years, encompassing significant institutional changes, particularly the development of financial intermediaries and a relative growth in "contractual" saving (life insurance and, later, amortization of mortgage payments as general practice) suggests that there are powerful and persistent forces making for constancy in savings shares. On this basis, therefore, we should expect pension fund saving not to lead to a change in a ratio that has persisted at about the same level for more than five decades. Rather, it would seem that accompanying the growth of pension funds, as with the rapidly burgeoning financial institutions of early periods, there should be an adjustment among savings media that would keep savings ratios approximately unchanged.

A resort to the "invisible hand" of empirical regularities never proves anything, of course. For here, too, as in the deductive argument presented earlier, to speak with certainty we need to know

---

[13] Raymond W. Goldsmith, *A study of Savings in the United States*, Vol. I, Princeton, Princeton University Press, 1955. Pp. 6-9.

how substitutable people consider pension savings to be, as against other forms of saving they might have undertaken. And there are good grounds, as Roger Murray notes, for holding that pension fund savings might be imperfect substitutes for a number of reasons:

1. The realization of full pension benefits may depend upon continuity of employment in the event of delayed or graded vesting.

2. An equity in a pension plan is illiquid. It cannot be drawn on, as can other forms of saving, in the interim period prior to retirement for other purposes.

3. Contributions to retirement programs are usually compulsory. As a result, the participant may have accumulated for his benefit sums well in excess of the amounts he would voluntarily save in any form. Workers employed at lower pay scales might, indeed, have their pension equities as virtually their only form of saving.[14]

In elaboration of the first reason we simply note that many workers are not in a position to be certain of pension receipts under the plan they are currently "covered" by, until they have been with the company a goodly number of years and/or have reached a fairly ripe age. Such is the nature of vesting requirements of private industrial plans. So, while some "big actuarial discounter up there" can be certain that what is accumulated in the way of assets each year by pension funds does represent obligations the plans will really incur, the effective saving, as perceived by individual participants and discounted additionally for their uncertainty, when summed up aggregates to considerably less than the annual growth in pension funds.

The second and third reasons given by Murray need no further explanation, but to his list I would add a fourth possibility, viz., that some workers may simply be ignorant of what is accumulating on their behalf. This is credible, given the demonstrated widespread lack of knowledge of much more direct and simple personal financial facts, e.g., marginal rates of income tax. It is also suggested by the results of a survey in Pennsylvania some years back, in which employers' records disclosed over 25 per cent more coverage than did employees' answers in a survey concerning this among other questions.[15]

---

14 Murray, *op. cit. supra* note 2, p. 55.
15 *Selected Employee Benefit Plans*, A Report of the Joint State Government Commission to the General Assembly of the Commonwealth of Pennsylvania, Session of 1955, Harrisburg, 1955. Pp. 15 and 39.

Both the deductive reasoning and the empirical evidence—prior to Cagan and Katona—suggest that if pension savings are reasonably good substitutes they will be at the expense of other saving virtually in full, and that if they are only imperfect substitutes total saving will increase because of pension saving, but by *less* than the amount of pension saving, except under the extreme assumption of zero substitutability. So we are left with the question: What really happens? Thanks to Cagan and Katona, we can answer this question. I shall concentrate on Cagan's work[16] in what follows.

Drawing on several surveys of a large sample of subscribers to Consumers Union, a consumer product testing and rating organization, Cagan was able to compare the savings behavior of households covered by private pension plans with those that were not. Replies from more than 11,000 households were used in establishing his major findings. Because the sample was so large, he was able, in effect, to standardize on other relevant dimensions and separate the effect of pension coverage per se.

Comparing simply households covered by pensions (8,008) and those not covered (2,911), he found that covered households had a saving ratio (a ratio of saving to income expressed as a per cent) of 11.5 per cent, compared with 7.7 per cent for noncovered households. Because the pension saving in the form of increases in their equity in pension plans was 2.8 per cent of income for the covered households, pension saving was clearly not at the expense of other saving. For covered households saved a higher fraction of income in all other forms than did households not covered by pensions [(11.5−2.8) > 7.7].[17]

As Cagan concludes, these data "indicate that coverage does not

16 Phillip Cagan, *The Effect of Pension Plans on Aggregate Saving*, New York, National Bureau of Economic Research, 1965, 97 p.

17 See *ibid.*, p. 21. Cagan divided personal savings into three categories: (1) discretionary (defined as the excess of the reported increase in cash and securities over the increase in nonmortgage debt), for which the covered and noncovered households had savings ratios of 2.8 and 2.1 per cent respectively; (2) other contractual (i.e., other than pension fund, hence reported increase in real estate and in equity and annuities), for which covered and noncovered households had savings ratios of 5.9 and 5.7 per cent respectively; and (3) pension saving, with covered households having a saving ratio of 2.8 per cent against the zero per cent for households not under pension plans. In all categories, therefore, covered households showed a higher propensity to save.

lead households to substitute their pension contributions for other forms of saving, but seems actually to induce a slight increase in other saving. If so, aggregate personal saving is increased by the amount of growth in pension funds and apparently also by a small amount of increased saving by covered households in other forms."[18]

But this conclusion so far rests simply on a gross separation of respondent households into those who are covered by private pension plans and those who are not. In fact, other variables are important determinants of saving, and it could well be that the two categories of households differ importantly with respect to these variables and that it is these differences that account for the observed difference in their savings ratios. Previous studies have demonstrated that the prime determinants of saving behavior are most likely income and age. Cagan, therefore, proceeded to "standardize" for those variables and then inquire as to whether the additional one—being covered by a pension or not—played a role in explaining observed differences in savings ratios among households similar as to both age and income class. The details of his statistical procedures do not concern us here; his conclusion does. On this more controlled basis, his previous conclusion was confirmed, and he ended up by asserting that "covered households make no net reductions in other forms of saving and in all likelihood make a net increase, though it may be less on the average than one percentage point."[19]

Not satisfied with simply establishing this finding, Cagan has subjected it to very critical scrutiny, first, to make certain that it is a "fact," by analyzing a number of other factors that could be "distorting" the data, and, second, to test various possible explanations of the effect he has found. His own explanation, summarized briefly (and in a form that hardly does justice to the extensive and careful job of hypothesis testing that he did), is as follows:

Pension coverage draws attention to the problems of providing for retirement and goes a long way in helping to solve them. It facilitates the rapidly spreading shift to financial means of providing for retirement from the older reliance on family, rental property, and the small family farm or business. But

---

18 See *ibid.*, p. 23.
19 See *ibid.*, p. 28.

by itself it is apparently found inadequate; the average household supplements it by additional accumulations, mostly in bank accounts and government bonds, at the expense of consumer durable purchases. I shall call this a "recognition" effect of coverage, for want of a better term.[20]

It is the "recognition" effect he sees as the explanation, and finds, from his research, good reason not to attribute the observed fact that pension savings are not made at the expense of other savings either to "unawareness or indifference" as regards pensions or to contradiction of the "proposition of economic theory that similar products are substitutes for each other."[21] Rather, he sees the effect of pension coverage as part of the adjustment taking place during a long period of sharp changes in saving forms from physical to financial assets.[22]

All that has been said, so far, relates to personal saving—only one of the three components of the total stream of saving. Business firms and governments also save, and the financial flows of pension plans can be expected to affect the saving of these two sectors and, hence, total saving. Here numerous "models" and tortuous chains of reasoning are possible. Cagan's treatment of this problem, while admittedly sketchy, nonetheless seems to cover the extremes of the reasonable range of possible results and concludes that only a small effect on business saving can be expected, while if the federal government attempts to recoup via taxation the revenues lost by the postponement of income tax on employers' contributions and the earnings of pension funds,[23] it could cut the net addition to savings that pension fund accumulations represent by no more than 20 per cent, and perhaps as little as 10 per cent.[24]

While interesting and significant, these findings about the effect of pensions on saving are based on the data of a very unrepresen-

---

[20] See *ibid.*, p. 53.

[21] See *ibid.*, pp. 82 and 86.

[22] See *ibid.*, p. 86, for the full explanation.

[23] An estimate of 1966 puts this revenue loss at $1.375 billion—compounded of a loss of $0.55 billion due to tax exemption of funds' earnings, a loss of $1.15 billion due to not taxing employers' contributions to the fund, and a gain of $0.325 billion from taxation of benefits received. See *Private Pension Plans*, Hearings before the Subcommittee on Fiscal Policy of the Joint Economic Committee, 89th Congress, 2nd Session, Part 2, Washington: Government Printing Office, May, 1966, p. 416.

[24] Cagan, *op. cit. supra* note 16, p. 80.

21

tative sample. The subscribers to Consumers Union are richer, more highly educated, and better informed than the average households. Of course, one could argue in all these respects that this sample, unrepresentative of United States households today, nonetheless has useful predictive value in that it is representative of what households will be like a decade or two hence. Be that as it may, it is not an argument that has to be relied upon. For findings similar to Cagan's in their import, derived also with great skill and ingenuity, and, in addition, based on three representative samples of American consumers (interviewed rather than, as for Cagan's sample, simply surveyed by mail), are to be found in George Katona's book, *Private Pensions and Individual Saving*.[25] While I have leaned much more heavily on Cagan's work, among other reasons because of its greater convenience for someone interested in generating numerical estimates, it is important that Katona, employing different data and techniques of investigation, reaches findings that are in the same ball park as Cagan's. According to Katona, "We conclude from the findings obtained by means of the new computer technique[26] that coverage by private pensions makes a difference in explaining saving performance, encouraging more saving rather than inhibiting it."[27]

It seems, therefore, that with more assurance than is generally possible about complex economic processes we may consider the annual growth in pension funds to represent net additions to the flow of personal saving and, after due allowance for possible offsets in corporate and government saving (or personal saving induced by government's attempt to maintain its revenues), to be

---

[25] George Katona, *Private Pensions and Individual Saving*, Ann Arbor, Survey Research Center, Institute for Social Research, The University of Michigan, 1965, 114 p. Some of the hypotheses tested and results similar to those reported appear in an earlier publication of Katona's, *The Mass Consumption Society*, New York, McGraw-Hill, 1964, 343 p.

[26] The reference here is to the Automatic Interaction Detector Program developed by two of Katona's colleagues at the Survey Research Center which "identifies that split of a sample into two subgroups which makes the greatest contribution toward explaining the total variation in the dependent variable. Then each of these subgroups is similarly examined for the best split, and so on." Therefore, "the sample is divided sequentially into that series of subgroups which maximizes one's ability to predict values of the dependent variable." (See Katona, *op. cit. supra* note 25—the first reference—pp. 81-82.)

[27] Katona, *op. cit. supra* note 25—the first reference—p. 88.

net additions to the annual flow of total saving to something like 80 to 90 per cent of the addition to pension fund assets. Moreover, both Katona and Cagan appear to agree that this type of response to participation in a pension plan, while not fixed for all time, is likely to remain of about the same order of magnitude for a goodly number of years into the future. The change in response that will come, they feel, will occur slowly.

The significance of this effect is a matter that can be assessed at a variety of levels. The highest level, the theory of appropriate or optimal rates of saving, is formidable at least and not particularly suitable for the discussion of such a mundane topic as pension saving per se. About this matter it suffices for our purposes to note that fiscal and monetary measures could be used to offset any imbalances between desired savings and investment opportunities.

On a simple and direct level, it seems quite appropriate that pension fund accumulation represent net new savings, for in this way the pension plans for individuals who are now working will permit capital formation during their working life that will be the basis for generating output to support them after retirement without digging into the output available for the advancing standard of living of the then working population. The answer to the question "Can we support the increasing burden of the aged population?" is a comfortable affirmative, if their pension plans provide additions to saving and if the community's desired saving is effectively invested.

This is not to suggest that there are not other ways of supporting the aged in retirement that would also make it something we can "afford." The presumption behind the government's pension program—OASDI—which is run virtually on a current basis, is that each retired generation can expect to be supported by the working generation, just as the former, when it worked, supported a retired generation. As stated earlier, this is a perfectly reasonable basis on which a national government can proceed. It does, however, point up another reason why the current effect of private pension programs on saving may be considered salutary. OASDI, essentially on a pay-as-you-go basis, exerts its economic effects via transfers of income through taxes on some to support benefit payments to others. Most students of this transfer process feel that it results in a decline in saving, because it involves redistribution from relatively high savers to relatively high spenders.[28] And since we rely both on OASDI and private pension plans for providing income support in old age, it seems fitting that private and public programs complement each other, the one tending to make saving lower than it would otherwise be, the other tending to raise saving over the level it would otherwise reach. Complementarity of this kind in economic effects is a healthy relationship (in the sense that "distortions" are less) and a strong argument for continuance of the combination of public and private mechanisms that make up our pension structure.[29]

The effect of pension plans in inducing net new saving can be considered salutary in another context, viz., to offset the decline in saving propensities observed in some other contexts, e.g., the decline in the saving component of life insurance in recent years.[30] Or, in a broader view of this problem, pension fund saving may be part of the answer to the important question raised in a capstone volume of a major study of capital formation in the United States by Simon Kuznets who noted factors in recent years (1948-57) tending to lower savings rates and, hence, keep "capital formation below the proportion required to increase productivity sufficiently to offset inflationary pressures."[31]

Finally, reverting to Table 4, note that in Roger Murray's judgment, pension fund saving has already played its most important role in the last several years and, while it is likely to increase over

---

28 See, for example, John J. Carroll, *Alternative Methods of Financing Old-Age, Survivors, and Disability Insurance*, Michigan Governmental Studies No. 38, Ann Arbor, Institute of Public Administration, University of Michigan, 1960, 187 p.

29 There are others as well, including the public arrangement's ability to provide a basic minimum for all and the ability of private plans to be adjusted more flexibly to particular preferences and circumstances. Needless to say, the choice between public or private arrangements or the relative weights of the two are complex problems about which these observations of mine should be viewed as ad hoc remarks, but not without relevance.

30 Perhaps it is because of declines in saving in other connections that the increase in pension savings has not been observed to date in national personal saving ratios. See Table 3.

31 Simon S. Kuznets, *Capital in the American Economy; Its Formation and Financing*, a study by the National Bureau of Economic Research, Princeton, Princeton University Press, 1961, p. 457.

the next decade, the relative importance of saving via pension funds will tend to decline. This shows up in the last three columns of the table.[32]

ECONOMIC EFFECTS: CAPITAL MARKETS

The private pension funds, whose annual asset accumulations for the purpose of the preceding section were lumped together, must be separated, in discussing their role in and implications for the capital markets. For each of the categories—private insured funds, private noninsured funds, and state-local employee funds— is a financial intermediary that operates under a particular set of objectives and constraints. And while, in the course of growth, increased sophistication and professionalization, along with legislative changes that remove some differential constraints, may cause them to become more similar, it is quite likely that sharp differences will remain in the financial assets they hold and in their portfolio preferences at the margin of choice. First, we shall look at the asset composition of each of the funds separately, and then at the assets for the aggregate of the three categories.

The assets of plans funded with insurance companies may be considered part and parcel (in the appropriate fraction) of the total of invested assets of insurance companies, which are tabulated in Table 5. Insured pension funds, of course, represent only a fraction of the assets listed in the table, but the proportions of different assets in insured pension funds' portfolios can be taken to be the same as in the "Percent of Total" column.[33]

Currently, the vast preponderance of insured pension fund holdings is in debt instruments, with corporate bonds and mortgages each about 41 per cent of the total, and government securities 8 per cent. Corporate stock and the miscellaneous category of other assets account for the remaining 10 per cent. Note par-

---

[32] For an elaboration of this point see pages 62 and 63 of the book from which the data of Table 4 were taken: Murray, *op. cit.,* supra note 2.

[33] Recent enabling legislation permitting insurance companies to set up segregated reserves for their pension funds and, in particular, to permit them to hold a much higher proportion of equities than in other life insurance company reserves, has not been in effect long enough to invalidate this statement. However, in the future one can expect rather sizable differences in the asset composition of insured pension fund reserves and the other reserves of insurance companies.

TABLE 5

ASSETS OF UNITED STATES LIFE INSURANCE COMPANIES, 1965, AND
CHANGE BETWEEN 1955 AND 1965

Assets	Amount (billions of dollars)	Per Cent of Total	Net Change Since 1955 (billions of dollars)	Per Cent of Net Change
Government securities[1]	11.5	8.0	— 0.3	— 0.5
Corporate bonds	58.6	40.5	22.7	37.0
Total bonds	70.1	48.5	22.4	36.5
Preferred stock	2.9	2.0	1.1	1.8
Common stock	6.3	4.3	4.4	7.2
Total stock	9.1	6.3	5.5	9.0
Mortgages	60.0	41.4	30.6	50.0
Other	5.7	3.9	2.7	4.4
Total	144.9	100.0	61.2	100.0

1 Includes United States, foreign and state, provincial, and local securities.

Source: Derived from Roger Murray, *Economic Aspects of Pensions: A Summary Report,* New York, National Bureau of Economic Research, 1968.

ticularly the small common stock percentage, which illustrates a competitive disadvantage that has in large part been legislatively lifted for insured pension plan reserves, but too recently to show up in the figures.[34] And, in fact, over the past decade we might also describe insured pension funds as dealing in debt, since the portfolio changes between 1955 and 1965 show a strong interest in mortgages, which accounted for half the increase in assets over the decade 1955-1965, and corporate bonds, in which close to 37 per cent of net fund additions went. That some portion of private industrial pension funds are heavy holders of debt instruments and, more pointedly, significant sources of funds in the mortgage and corporate bond markets, is important to note, since the fact tends to get swamped by the interest and concern with noninsured funds' holdings and rate of acquisition of common stock.

---

34 The prospective return on common stock and the desire to "hedge" a fund with assets that move with the price level (since pressures to modify benefit payments to keep up with prices are strong, and, in fact, an increasing number of plans gear benefits to final as contrasted with average pay) make equities attractive assets for pension funds, and help to explain the relatively more rapid growth of noninsured as against insured funds. In 1940, insured funds had assets of $1 billion and noninsured, $1.4 billion; by 1965, their reserves stood at $27.3 billion and $58.1 billion respectively.

This is highlighted by the data of Table 6. Given the composition of their assets, noninsured private pension funds might currently be described as holders of corporate securities, with common stock accounting for almost half their total assets and bonds well over a third. Together, they make up over 82 per cent of the investment portfolio of private noninsured funds. (Were assets valued at market rather than book, common stock alone would be well above 50 per cent.) But as the percentages for the change in the most recent period indicate, their attention has been heavily concentrated on common stock, which represents well over half the additions to assets in these nine years, and heavily also, but to a lesser degree, on corporate bonds, in which they put a little more than one-fourth of net accumulation. They are still not an important force in the mortgage market, but seem to be moving into it to a greater extent. While present holdings of common stock constitute a small fraction of stock outstanding, private noninsured funds' rate of acquisition relative to net new issues is very high, exceeding 100 per cent in the last several years. Moreover, while currently their holdings are relatively small, with noninsured pension funds continuing to expand buoyantly, and with a major fraction of the expansion continuing to go into net acquisitions

TABLE 6

ASSETS OF PRIVATE NONINSURED PENSION FUNDS,[1] 1967, AND
CHANGE BETWEEN 1958 AND 1967

Assets	Book Value (billions of dollars)	Per Cent of Total	Net Change in Book Value Since 1958 (billions of dollars)	Per Cent of Net Change
Cash and deposits	1.2	1.7	0.7	1.5
United States government securities	2.2	3.1	— 0.4	— 0.9
Corporate bonds	25.5	35.5	12.7	27.3
Preferred stock	1.0	1.4	0.2	0.4
Common stock	33.9	47.2	27.1	58.3
Mortgages	3.9	5.4	3.2	6.9
Other	4.1	5.7	3.1	6.7
Total	71.8	100.0	46.5	100.0

[1] Includes funds of nonprofit organizations and multi-employer plans.
Source: United States Securities and Exchange Commission, Statistical Bulletin, July 1968, and Annual Releases.

TABLE 7

ASSETS OF STATE AND LOCAL GOVERNMENT EMPLOYEE RETIREMENT
SYSTEMS, 1967, AND CHANGE BETWEEN 1957[a] AND 1967[a]

Assets	Amount (billions of dollars)	Per Cent of Total Assets	Net Change Since 1957 (billions of dollars)	Per Cent of Net Change
Cash and deposits	0.4	1.0	0.2	0.7
Federal government securities	6.7	17.1	1.6	6.1
State and local government securities	2.4	6.1	— 0.9	— 3.4
Corporate bonds	20.3	51.8	16.9	64.3
Corporate stock	2.4	6.1	2.2	8.4
Mortgages	4.8	12.2	4.3	16.3
Other	2.2	5.6	2.0	7.6
Total	39.2	100.0	26.3	100.0

[a] Fiscal year.

Source: U.S. Department of Commerce, Bureau of the Census, *Employee-Retirement Systems of State and Local Governments,* 1967 Census of Governments, Volume 6, p. 11.

of common stock, the stock ownership of noninsured pension funds could take on much greater importance.

Now we round out the picture with consideration of assets of pension plans for employees of state and local governments. (See Table 7.) It was observed that these funds experience sizable and increasing annual growth and can be expected to do so for a considerable period into the future. Currently, their assets consist almost wholly of debt claims, and given the institutional environment and constraints under which they operate, a major portion of assets in this form is likely to continue. But there has been very pronounced change in the relative importance of the debt instruments they hold. In part this represents the growing sophistication of the management of such funds—a distinct movement toward professionalization—and in part it expresses the response of professional managers, or indeed the interest of anyone who seeks to maximize benefits, given contributions, (or to minimize contributions, given benefits), in obtaining the highest return, duly qualified, of course, for risk. Thus corporate bonds now comprise over half the assets of state-local employee funds; over the most recent decade close to two-thirds of the additions to these funds have taken this form. Over this same period a not inconsequential amount of mortgages has been taken up and a relatively small amount of common stock. As to government securities, there has been some growth in federal and a slight decline in state and local. In 1957, state-local employee funds might aptly have been described as holders of government debt. By 1967, their major holding was corporate bonds, with government securities still an important, but by now secondary, area of investment.

As noted above, however, there are good reasons to believe that state-local funds will remain heavily and primarily in debt instruments. Thus, Roger Murray feels that

> It is doubtful that state and local retirement systems will soon break out of the statutory, accounting, and institutional restraints on their effective management of huge aggregations of capital. While the high cost of pension benefits will create increasing pressure to improve rates of return, it is not likely that the public systems will greatly accelerate the pace at which they follow private funds. Nor is it likely that they will be as flexible in approaching investment opportunities as they occur in the future of a dynamic capital market structure.[35]

While it may, therefore, be a matter of some concern that increasingly large amounts of funds will be funneled through a relatively inflexible financial institution, there is basis for a more sanguine view when the future direction of fund flows of state-local plans is assessed in conjunction with the asset acquisitions of the pension funds for individuals in private employment. For altogether the structure of pension fund flows could, because of a complementary relation among its component parts, provide for a more suitable matching of fund sources and uses than if the pattern characteristic of private or state-local alone predominated. Table 8, which draws on estimates made by Roger Murray of possible future dimensions of particular types of asset acquisitions by pension funds for those in private employment and for those in the employment of state and local governments, is an attempt to point up the complementarity and, more generally, allay, to some degree at least, concern about imbalances between the types of financial assets that pension funds may seek to acquire and those that the various entities who seek funds would wish to offer. To understand how these estimates were derived and, therefore, whether he is in general agreement

---

[35] Murray, *op. cit. supra* note 2, p. 110. See pp. 109-110 for the basis for his conclusion.

TABLE 8

POSSIBLE FUTURE NET PURCHASES OF FINANCIAL ASSETS BY
PRIVATE PENSION FUNDS AND STATE-LOCAL EMPLOYEE FUNDS
(SELECTED DATES, 1965-1980)

Type of Financial Asset	1965ᵃ				1970			
	Net Purchase (billions of dollars)			Per Cent of Total Financial Asset Purchases	Net Purchase (billions of dollars)			Per Cent of Total Financial Asset Purchases
	Private	State-Local	Total		Private	State-Local	Total	
Government securities	—0.5	—0.4	— 0.9	— 8.8	b.	—0.2	— 0.2	— 1.7
Corporate bonds	2.2	2.3	4.5	44.1	1.3	2.0	3.3	28.2
Corporate stock	3.3	0.4	3.7	36.3	4.3	0.9	5.2	44.4
Mortgages	1.6	0.6	2.7	21.6	1.6	1.0	2.6	22.2
Other	0.3	0.4	0.7	6.9	0.3	0.5	0.8	6.8
Total	6.9	3.3	10.2	100.0	7.5	4.2	11.7	100.0

ᵃ Actual data from Federal Reserves Flow of Funds Accounts, and not strictly comparable with data in Table 3.

ᵇ Negligible.

Source: Roger F. Murray, *Economic Aspects of Pensions: A Summary Report,* New York,

with them, the interested reader must go to Murray's book.[36]
Looking at the Total row in Table 8, we can see the projected
more rapid rate of accumulation for state-local funds, providing
an increased amount and growing proportion of total pension
fund accumulation—from less than one-third of the total in 1965
to well over half by 1980. After 1970, it would appear that state-
local plans will be responsible for almost all of the annual increase
in pension fund accumulation.[37] For complementarities within par-

---

[36] See *ibid.* at pp. 86-97 and 110-115. The reader will discover that I have taken
great liberties with Murray's numbers, have spliced some together, and in general
have rearranged and composed categories in a way that someone more cognizant
of the particularities of their derivation would have been reluctant to do. But
Murray's picture of possibilities seems reasonable to me, and thus Table 8, even
with the numerous caveats that my operations on his data add to his own, is useful
for illustrative or indicative purposes.

I will not list here all sources of potential mayhem on Murray's figures, but must
note that in Table 8 the category of Government Securities, in plans for those in
private employment, is the sum of United States government securities and state
and local obligations, taken from Murray's Table 12 for 1965, added to the Government Securities item in Table 13 for the other years, while for state-local funds, it
is the sum of United States government securities and state and local government
securities, as shown in his Table 16.

[37] This would be a real possibility even if, as is likely, the projections on which
Murray's estimates are based (i.e., those in Daniel M. Holland's *Private Pension
Funds: Projected Growth*) understate the level of the accumulations of the funds for
those in private employment.

TABLE 8 (Continued)

Type of Financial Asset	1975 Net Purchase (billions of dollars)			Per Cent of Total Financial Asset Purchases	1980 Net Purchase (billions of dollars)			Per Cent of Total Financial Asset Purchases
	Private	State-Local	Total		Private	State-Local	Total	
Government securities	0.2	0.2	0.4	2.9	0.2	0.4	0.6	3.7
Corporate bonds	1.9	2.5	4.4	32.6	2.4	3.1	5.5	33.7
Corporate stock	3.0	1.4	4.4	32.4	2.0	2.5	4.5	27.6
Mortgages	2.0	1.3	3.3	24.3	2.2	2.0	4.2	25.8
Other	0.5	0.6	1.1	8.1	0.6	0.9	1.5	9.2
Total	7.6	6.0	13.6	100.0	7.4	8.9	16.3	100.0

National Bureau of Economic Research, 1968, pp. 86, 93, and 112. In assembling this table I have added together some of Murray's categories in a not wholly warranted fashion and have used data not strictly comparable. I have inserted none of Murray's caveats nor any explanation of his methods and assumptions. Consequently, the estimates are at best suggestive.

ticular categories of financial assets, if the possibilities of Table 8 are valid, it would be state-local funds that would first cushion the decline in the pension fund sector's net demand for corporate bonds and then raise it to higher absolute levels, although, relative to other financial assets, the demand will not get as high as in 1965. As for corporate stock, about which there is much concern relative to the "disproportionate" acquisitions by pension funds,[38] Murray's possibilities show funds for individuals in private employment tending to be less vigorous in this direction after five or ten years, and state-local funds showing somewhat more interest. On net balance for the aggregate of both categories of funds, however, a steadying-down of the amount of such purchases is indicated, with a decline in their relative proportion among financial instruments acquired. As to the third major category of financial assets—mortgages—the future could very well see increased absolute amounts of purchase by both private and state-local funds,

---

[38] As Murray notes, some of this concern, focussed, say, on the statistic that the noninsured pension funds for those in private employment have annually made net new purchases of stock greater than (sometimes many multiples greater than) net new issues of common stock, fails first to net out investment company purchases, but more importantly fails to recognize (1) that corporate retentions are net new issues de facto and pension fund purchases fall far short of them, and (2) that an addition to the supply of equities is forthcoming each year from the estates of wealthy persons to help meet taxes thereon. (See Murray, op. cit. supra, note 2, pp. 87-88.)

and, therefore, a relative rise in the importance of mortgages among assets acquired annually.

Whether this is a "good" pattern or a "bad" pattern depends on many things beyond our purview. But on the basis of Alfred Marshall's faith that economic processes are orderly—*natura non facit saltum*—the tendency of these two sets of funds to balance off in financial asset preferences could very well be salutary.

Because the future is, of course, uncertain, and because, therefore, pension funds for those in private employment might purchase stock more heavily than the possibilities incorporated in Table 8, Roger Murray has also estimated their holdings should they continue to put as much as 60 per cent of annual net accumulations into equities on up through 1980.[39] Should they do this, their holdings would have a market value of $182 billion by 1980 and, by the same assumption of market value growth (five per cent per annum—Murray, *op. cit.*, page 93) the total market value of stock outstanding—$675 billion in 1965—would be $1,418 billion by 1980. Thus pension funds for those in private employment (state-local holdings will still be small enough not to make much difference in our conclusion) would still own less than 14 per cent of common stock outstanding.

Many would argue, however, that directing attention to aggregate holdings misses an important element of the problem, i.e., the danger of concentration of control, for pension funds, and other institutional investors, have a penchant for purchasing from among a relatively small group of stocks. While this is undeniable, there is little data and even less time to pursue this question. We know that

. . . as of 1954, noninsured pension funds under trusteeship of New York banks (about half, by value, of all noninsured funds) held more than 3 per cent of stock outstanding in only 17 companies, and in only three of these instances did their ownership exceed 5 per cent. Also, of the ten stocks in which their total absolute holdings were greatest, they held on the average, only 1 per cent of shares outstanding.[40]

---

[39] These, as his other possibilities, do not distinguish between insured and noninsured funds since, as Murray points out, recent changes in legislation permit insured pension funds wide latitude in the amounts and proportions of equities they can hold.

[40] Daniel M. Holland, "Pension Funds" in *International Encyclopedia of the Social Sciences*, Volume 11, New York, Crowell Collier and Macmillan, 1968, p. 526.

But a lot of water since then has "run over the pension dam" (or should we say, continuing the analogy used earlier, "risen in the pension bathtub") and will continue to do so.

Common sense provides some grounds for comfort here, however. Lintner notes that pension fund trustees would be expected to search for alternatives, should their "favorites' " yield be bid too high.[41] And it is well known, too, that the list of "favorites" changes greatly over time. Also, those companies whose stocks are heavily in demand are likely to increase their supply. All this does not mean, however, that there is no cause for concern, nor need for developing mechanisms to pass through to individuals the voting rights on the stock held by pension funds.[42] The Sears Roebuck experience alone suggests this.

As to the effect of pension fund accumulations on stock prices, Murray concludes that

> Neither the proposition that pension funds bid up the share prices for a limited group of "institutional favorites" nor the proposition that they are contributing to price volatility in selected shares can be supported by available evidence. On the contrary, it appears that portfolio managers are broadening their range of investment alternatives and taking advantage of the long time horizon implicit in their decisions.[43]

The "long time horizon" however, does suggest the possibility that institutionalization could raise the general level of stock prices. For the investment decision involves a trade-off between risk (variability) and return. If the long-time investor (the institution) does not see as much risk in connection with the variability of a given stock as does the individual whose period of holding may be less predictable, then the institution would be willing to pay more than the individual for a claim to a given income stream.

---

[41] John Lintner, "The Financing of Corporations," in Edward S. Mason, editor, *The Corporation in Modern Society*, Cambridge, Harvard University Press, 1959, p. 199.

[42] Some important and stimulating references on this problem are: Paul P. Harbrecht, *Pension Funds and Economic Power*, New York, Twentieth Century Fund, 1959, 328 p.; Robert Tilove, *Pension Funds and Economic Freedom*, New York, Fund for the Republic, 1959, 91 p.; and Dwayne Wrightsman, "Pension Funds and Economic Concentration," *Quarterly Review of Economics and Business*, 7 (Winter, 1967).

[43] Murray, *op. cit. supra* note 2, pp. 90-91.

CHAPTER II

THE EFFECTS OF TAXATION OF EXECUTIVE COMPENSATION ON ECONOMIC ACTIVITY

DAN THROOP SMITH
Professor of Finance,
Harvard Graduate School of Business Administration

MANAGEMENT is increasingly recognized as a distinct and important factor of production, along with labor, capital, and natural resources. For too long and in too many places, management has been regarded as just another form of labor, specialized to be sure but not fundamentally different from other types of work calling for distinctive talents.

Effective management, in fact, not only operates along with the other factors of production. It plays a key role in taking the initiative in bringing them together in the right places and the right proportions, to use the right technologies to produce and sell the right goods and services.

IMPORTANCE OF EFFECTIVE MANAGEMENT

In our dynamic world, effective management must involve a considerable amount of entrepreneurship. Successful top management requires innovation. It is not simply the supervision of work under established rules. Management as used here covers the activities of the higher levels of executives in widely-owned corporations and of owner-managers and any senior salaried executives in closely controlled companies.

The effectiveness of management is in many respects more dependent on their attitudes and objectives than on the amount of time or the intensity of their efforts. This is a distinctive feature of

34

management activity in comparison to that of most other forms of productive activity where output is related to time and intensity of effort so long as it stops well short of fatigue. Effective managers, to be sure, usually work long hours; their jobs often involve round-the-clock and round-the-calendar preoccupations, as their wives and families readily testify. But this intensity is a reflection of personal temperament and is not essential to success. It may even make more difficult the development of perspective and new ideas.

Recent self-criticism of the industrial systems in Europe testifies to the importance of imaginative and wise innovation and risk-taking as one of the principal strengths in the American economy. A comparison is often made with management traditions elsewhere which involve too much of a caretaker point of view with an attempt to minimize apparent risks, with a result that the major risk of obsolescence is involuntarily incurred. The importance of management in a dynamic economy should need no further elaboration.

Lest it be thought that the foregoing comments represent a naive acceptance of the idea that a completely free market economy will lead to ideal results, it should of course be noted that controls are necessary to prevent the promotion of products which are harmful personally or socially. Vastly greater restrictions than we now have must be adopted to prevent physical and aesthetic pollution of the environment through the processes of production. Standards of competition must be established and maintained to prevent the development of monopolies with excessive prices and a possible slowing of innovation. But subject to these constraints, and with sensible policies and attitudes to prevent population growth from swamping all possible gains, the importance of effective management in improving economic well-being seems well recognized.

The topic under discussion here is the relation of the tax treatment of executive compensation to economic activity. The tax law produces its effect through its influence on the attitudes of executives and the direction of their attention and activities, as well as its influence on the supply of executive talent through the choice of careers.

35

As a general proposition, it seems fair to say that in an ideal compensation system the personal pecuniary interests of executives should coincide with the long-run development of the companies they manage and that long-term profitable growth, when it is based on efficient use of resources and successful innovation, is in the interests of those involved in the business, whether as employees, owners, suppliers, or customers, and the nation. To help secure this goal, the tax treatment of executive compensation should give preference to, or at least not penalize, compensation plans which reward long-term profitable growth. By this standard, our tax laws are certainly not helpful and in many ways are perverse.

Non-Pecuniary Incentives

Before examining the impact of the tax laws on various forms of executive compensation, one should note the significance of non-pecuniary incentives for executives. A successful executive has many satisfactions quite unrelated to his monetary rewards. Prestige, power, and a sense of personal achievement through the assumption and exercise of responsibility are all strong positive factors. If a person is to be a successful executive, he probably has an inherent taste for the role and perhaps a sense of frustration if he does not have a chance to employ his talents in that direction. Certainly the choice among careers and employment is not primarily influenced by material rewards for those who aspire to do more than routine work as a means of livelihood. The pecuniary rewards of executives must be seen in perspective, but they cannot be ignored. The effects of taxation must be considered in this setting.

Effect of High Individual Tax Rates

The first observation concerning taxation is that very high individual tax rates largely nullify the significance of ordinary compensation in the form of annual salaries for top executives. It has been virtually impossible to maintain a real net income after taxes under the combined impact of inflation and high marginal tax rates over the past 40 years under any conceivable increases in salaries. This fact has been shown by numerous calculations. The current surcharge on the individual income tax gives a good example of the exaggerated effect of high taxes. It raised the top rate from 70 to 77 per cent, thereby reducing net income at the margin from 30 to 23 cents on the dollar. It would take a salary increase of 30 per cent to maintain the net income at the top level, while at the bottom tax rate, where net incomes were reduced from 86 to 84.6 cents on the dollar, a wage increase of less than 2 per cent would more than cover the new tax burden.

The high rates of individual taxation inevitably divert personal attention from attempts to earn more income to attempts to reduce taxes. This fact cannot fail to direct attention away from productive work.

Pensions and deferred compensation contracts are of greater importance to executives than they would be if marginal tax rates were lower. Any shift of taxability of income from higher to lower tax brackets increases its net value. The advantages of postponement from a tax standpoint must of course be set against the present-value disadvantage and the opportunity cost of foregoing the chance to make an immediate investment in an inflationary economy. The advantages of postponement often more than offset the postponement of receipt, as is manifest from the interest in participation in qualified pension plans and in individual deferred compensation contracts. The tax law is relatively liberal with respect to both forms of postponement, though the proposed new regulations regarding the integration of pension benefits with social security seem needlessly complex. They attempt to introduce a perfectionist approach in one small segment of a system which is inherently crude and imperfect. Hopefully, good sense will prevail and the requirements will at least be continued along familiar lines which are themselves sufficiently complicated to discourage the adoption of pension plans in small companies.

Effect on Mobility of Management

From the standpoint of public policy, it is questionable whether the arrangements to postpone receipt of income do not seriously reduce the mobility of management talent and keep many executives from moving into positions where their talents would be most productive. Desirable though private provision for retirement income is from a social standpoint, there may be significant disadvantages from the standpoint of economic efficiency. Even for individual companies, the advantages of holding needed executives may be offset by the disadvantages of having unneeded executives hold on to jobs, to secure pensions, instead of moving on to other companies. Deferred compensation contracts, in contrast to pensions, are often used to move executives who forego non-vested pension benefits with an existing employer. To some extent, at least, they probably increase mobility and efficiency.

It is not, I believe, naive to say that the attitudes and policies of an enlightened owner-manager, concerned about the long-run value of his company and operating under appropriate constraints of law and public opinion, are likely to be socially as well as privately useful. In saying this I emphasize the word "enlightened" and again note the need for constraints. The advantage comes from a true interest in long-term values which requires attention to innovation, efficiency, and continued acceptance by employees and customers.

Stock Options

Under the present high tax rates it is virtually impossible for executives to save enough to buy really significant amounts of stock in the companies they manage. Stock options have been an alternative way of providing and securing a proprietary interest for salaried executives; they were used long before the tax laws made them especially attractive for tax reasons.

Unfortunately, stock options have been abused in too many cases by what are little more than grab-and-run tactics. To the extent that an option is exercised and the stock soon sold at capital gain rates, no significant long-term point of view is developed in the participating executives. In fact, emphasis may be concentrated on short-run action to increase stock prices, and this may be at the expense of action which would improve long-run values. Just as a profit-sharing plan, though sound in principle, may detract from research and development work which has no near-term prospect of improving profits, a stock option plan in which realization of short-term gains is tolerated may be actually perverse in its effect. The tax treatment of stock options unfortunately not only permits relatively quick realization of gain. In spite of the recent lengthening of the holding period, it has focused attention on the near term by reducing the period over which options can run, from 10 to 5 years. A review of the law in this area seems appropriate.

It is perhaps too much to expect companies to impose more stringent requirements on special compensation devices than those specified in the tax law. For that reason it might be worth considering a requirement for qualification that on any sale of stock within 10 years the company has the right to repurchase it at original issue price. This would limit the use of options when loans are necessary to purchase and carry stock, but a change of this sort may be necessary to put options on a basis such that the tax treatment is largely confined to instances in which the desired objective of emphasis on a long-term proprietary point of view is reinforced.

Use of Restricted Stock

In the meantime, there is increasing interest in the use of restricted stock. The subject needs more attention from the standpoint of public policy. It may be that the periods over which restrictions run are more conducive to a long look ahead on the part of executives. But the bargain purchases in the sales at less than market price raise interesting analytical problems in comparing net advantages to optionees with net costs to companies. In at least some instances, the apparent advantages in the use of restricted stock do not stand up under analysis. (A new and tighter Treasury position regarding income derived from restricted stock will probably greatly reduce its use in executive compensation.)

Mergers and Their Significance

In recent years there has apparently been an accelerating activity in mergers, many of which appear to be founded more on immediate financial benefits than on operating economies, however broadly this may be defined. Many mergers do increase efficiency. They may rescue failing businesses or provide for continuity when an owner-manager group retires or dies. Mergers may be the best way to provide funds for expansion, or access to technology or markets. They may even increase competition by strengthening smaller units.

But many mergers occur because of the great advantages which a company whose stock is selling at a very high price-earnings ratio can offer, and receive, through mergers. The owners of the acquired company receive an increase in value, though a reduction in earnings per share, and the stockholders of the acquiring company secure an increase in earnings per share which helps to maintain or even increase the high price-earnings ratio. This elementary basis for mergers is built upon and compounded in many ingenious ways through the use of senior securities and new possibilities of leverage based on newly-acquired debt capacity or the use of relatively idle liquid assets.

The real economic significance of mergers in terms of their effect on economic efficiency has never been rigorously examined. The typical analysis has been in terms of concentration in industry, because this has been the criterion for enforcement of antitrust policy. But concentration is not a criterion for economic efficiency and perhaps not a very good one even for probable competition.

We need to know more about the effects of mergers on company policies and executive attitudes. To what extent does a new availability of funds remove an impediment to expansion and reduce frustration? To what extent does a new headquarters staff create annoyance, impair vitality, and create frustration? These are among the elusive facts on which some knowledge is needed to appraise the significance of mergers.

But the subject here is taxation, and the question is how it influences the merger movement. A few points are familiar. The opportunity for tax-free mergers gives an advantage to that form of disposition of a company over a sale to a new group of owners who will continue it as a separate entity. (The recent Treasury ruling regarding special forms of stock will only slightly impede mergers; the special issues were used as sweeteners rather than essential elements in a merger offer.) The loss carry-over provisions do not impede mergers; they are, in fact, necessary to maintain substantial neutrality between mergers and continued existence of independent companies.

Perhaps the greatest tax factor in mergers is the great opportunity for personal gain which they present. Quick fortunes seem to be more readily available through mergers than through a solid building of a single company. And in too many cases mergers may be parasitic and even predatory. To the extent that they are not constructive, the most enthusiastic supplier of private enterprise must not ignore them or their effects. In fact, those who are most anxious to support the system should be the most vigorous to prevent abuses. Especially among the large numbers of uncommitted young people, spectacular examples of successful wheeling-dealing can only confirm suspicions that business is predatory.

It is by no means clear how much the tax premiums on successful maneuvers divert attention away from constructive management. Perhaps the wheeler-dealers are as they are by temperament and would pursue their present line of activities for the fun of the game. But it does seem unfortunate that the tax system gives them greater economic rewards and to some extent swells their ranks with those who under a neutral system of rewards would in the most literal sense of the term stick to their own businesses.

ESTABLISHMENT OF NEW VENTURES

At the other end of the life cycle of business concerns, our tax law is quite favorable, probably the best in the world. The establishment of new companies is facilitated by numerous provisions ranging from the nonrecognition of gain on incorporation to section 1244 and subchapter S, which in different ways permit favorable treatment of losses in new ventures, thereby encouraging investment in them. It is also possible for executives to receive substantial pecuniary rewards from participation in new companies.

The continual creation of new concerns is an element of strength in our economy. They frequently are the source of innovation and provide, in the phrase of the late Sumner Slichter, additional "centers of initiative." It is not clear to what extent the possibility of greater financial gain is a principal inducement for able young men to establish and join new ventures. To a large extent it is a preference for greater responsibility and the chance to exercise initiative—in short, a way of life—that is appealing. But at least our tax law is helpful. It could be made even better if some of the limitations imposed as a matter of caution in section 1244 and subchapter S when they were developed a little over a decade ago were now relaxed.

Other countries, incidentally, might do well to review their own tax laws from the standpoint of their influence on the establishment of new ventures. To be sure, a favorable tax climate will not change a traditional preference for employment in the civil service or with large corporations, but it might help. A well-publicized modification of the tax law might stimulate entrepreneurial imagination.

In recent years, a proposal has been advanced in several companies that it would be desirable to give greater autonomy to the executives responsible for separate divisions of a large corporation and to tie in their compensation with performance in more fundamental ways than bonuses related to budgets or departmental profit-sharing plans. The creation of separate corporations might also facilitate financing. An obvious way to establish this new form of industrial organization would be by partial spin-offs. These are, however, virtually precluded by the present tax law.

Spin-offs have been a source of abuse in the past when they were used to siphon off earnings at capital gains tax rates, and partial spin-offs must be regarded as inherently suspect. But the business and economic advantages of greater independence seem sufficiently great to justify a re-examination of the law. Perhaps under prescribed conditions a one-time partial spin-off might be permitted to establish a new pattern of industrial evolution, with an increase in the number of centers of initiative.

SUGGESTED SOLUTIONS

The points of criticism regarding the tax treatment of executive compensation, explicit or implied, are numerous. The solutions are less clear. The most obvious and probably the most beneficial change would be a reduction in the top bracket rates in the individual income tax. This would reduce the relative advantage now given to forms of compensation which at times lead to action of questionable economic and social advantage. A reduction in the top bracket rates would have only minor impact on the revenue and might, in fact, increase it as attention was turned again to truly productive activities.

A review of the tax treatment of deferred compensation and stock options in the light of their impact on executive mobility and activities would be useful.

Finally, the influence of our tax laws on the structure of our industry needs a thoughtful and critical analysis. Too frequently, tax policy has been set in too narrow a framework of goals. Small business always has a strong sentimental appeal, and this is probably a good thing, though in some small business programs sentiment has gotten the better of good sense. We have not had occasion, however, to review the whole tax system from the standpoint of its effect on our industrial pattern. Because of the differential tax treatment of various forms of executive compensation, along with many other tax factors, the tax laws may operate to encourage an industrial structure that is far from ideal from the standpoint of a dynamic economy.

PART TWO

HOW TAXES AFFECT BENEFIT PLANS FOR
EMPLOYEES GENERALLY

"Within the general theme of the symposium, this session is intended to increase our understanding of the benefits which have been influenced by our tax laws. We shall concentrate on social insurance and the broadly based benefits which supplement it. By broadly based, I mean those usually applicable to all classes of employees. In later sessions benefits for salaried employees and executives will be discussed.

"Perhaps it will be helpful to you if I state briefly two personal conclusions about the effect of taxes on the benefits we shall be discussing. My purpose is to provide a frame of reference as you follow our discussion.

"First, these pensions and benefits would be needed and would exist to a large extent if there were no tax benefits connected with them. They contain elements of insurance which make them highly desirable from a social as well as an individual viewpoint. I recall having rather heated discussions 20 years ago with a rugged individualist who disapproved on principle of social security and pensions. Unfortunately, when he became 55, and before he could carry out his personal savings program to completion, he became ill and unable to work any more. His disapproval of pension and benefit protection then vanished.

"There are also business reasons for having benefit and pension plans, to make possible the maintenance of an effective and vital work force. The Bell System companies, for instance, adopted such plans in 1913, before the federal income tax, personal or corporate, was a factor to be considered. So I disagree emphatically with the school of thought which attributes the entire existence of these plans to favorable tax treatment.

"My second point, on the other hand, is that without question the *form* of these benefits has been influenced to some extent by our tax laws. Congress obviously could destroy them, if it wished, by imposing taxes. And Congress has influenced them by tax penalties in some areas. Also, and particularly with respect to employee contributions, our tax laws have encouraged and are encouraging noncontributory plans of all kinds. Whether that is good or bad, with respect to particular types of plans, is highly debatable.

"Thus, within the field of taxes, which is your primary interest, there are important questions relating to these benefits. Our hope at this session is to further your acquaintance with the benefit plans themselves, and to identify tax effects upon them.

"Since your speakers will not cover medical expense benefits, I shall undertake to do so, very briefly.

"Employers for many years have been able to pay for the medical expenses of their employees, and to pay insurance premiums to cover such expenses, treating the payments as a business expense. Further, the employer payments are not treated as "income" to the employee. This tax situation has added to the desire of employees to have their employers pay for these expenses, in before-tax dollars. For instance, in a personal discussion with a representative of a large union, I said I thought sharing of the cost of medical expense premiums by employees is healthy. He said the leaders of his union agreed, but the rank and file did not, the clinching argument in their minds being the tax advantage when the employer pays the whole cost.

"Last year the federal Income Tax Law permitted individuals a deduction equal to one-half of the medical expense insurance premiums they paid. This removes half of the tax incentive to have the employer pay the whole cost. Of course, it also helps those who do not have employers, and restores a measure of tax equity. But I expect the remaining tax incentive will continue to exert pressure in the direction of "employer-pay-all" arrangements.

"Carrying this further, however, the American Medical Association a couple of months ago made a sweeping tax suggestion, as some of you may know. The A.M.A.'s suggestion is that health insurance premiums operate as a partial payment of individual income taxes, in other words, a credit against the tax due, and, further, that the government reimburse the individual for a premium amount paid in excess of the credit he could take.

"I am not prepared to discuss this, but it is further evidence, if any is needed, that taxes and benefits are intimately related."

—Robert E. Royes
Secretary, Employees Benefit Committee,
American Telephone and Telegraph Company

CHAPTER III

RELATIVE IMPORTANCE OF SOCIAL SECURITY AND PRIVATE PENSION PLANS

Alvin M. David

Assistant Commissioner for Program Evaluation and Planning, United States Social Security Administration

IF I WERE to take literally the subject on which I was asked to talk, I am afraid I would have very little to say. I would say that both social security and private pension plans are important. And as to their relative importance, my only contribution is to say that social security is bigger and pays out more money. However, I can say some other things if you will allow me to depart somewhat from a literal interpretation of my subject as stated on the program.

ADVANTAGES OF SOCIAL SECURITY

Social security does have certain advantages over most private plans. For example, it can be carried from one job to another. It is not subject to the risk of an employer going out of business, or running into financial difficulties, as a private plan might be. Also, by reason of social security being a government plan and being compulsory, it can be financed safely on a pay-as-you-go basis.

Moreover, as wages and productivity go up, the income to the social security system goes up, because contributions are a percentage of wages. With the higher income, it is possible to pay higher benefits—benefits that are geared fairly closely to the current level of income—without changing the contribution rate.

Social security, then, has the advantage that it can be kept up-to-date and the benefits can be raised from time to time without raising the contribution rates.

The social security contribution rates have been raised over the years, but along with these increases have gone major extensions and improvements in the system, which have increased its cost. For instance, benefits for survivors, benefits for dependents, benefits for disabled workers, and, lately, benefits for medical expenses in old age have been added to the original system.

It seems to me—although this is arguable, I am sure—that the existence of social security has stimulated the development of private plans; that is, up to now, at least, the more that people have had in the way of basic security through the social security program, the more they have become interested in the subject and the more they have seen the desirability of supplementation. If there had not been a social security system—and I am saying this irrespective of all the various tax laws and tax incentives—probably, I think, there would not have been as big a development of private plans as there has been.

What Social Security Is

I should like to say a word about what social security is and what it is not, because from all the experiences I have had, I know that there has been a great deal of misunderstanding about social security. While you are a sophisticated audience, you do get exposed to some things in the press and elsewhere on which it may be worthwhile for me to let you know that there are more and different things to be said on the subject.

Social security is a system of social insurance. I don't really care to worry about the name that you call it, or whether you are in agreement that it is any kind of insurance at all. We in the Social Security Administration call it a system of social insurance, and by the "insurance" part of that term we mean that employees and employers and self-employed people put money into a fund, and if the risk occurs that this system is set up to deal with—that is, if earnings are lost because the person retires or becomes disabled or dies—money is paid out of the fund to those who have incurred the earnings loss.

Not a Tax System

Social security is not a tax system, or not just a tax system. There is a social security tax, referred to in the law as a "Federal Insurance Contribution." But it is not simply a tax. The employee pays in, and as a result of his paying in he is going to draw some benefits, and by and large the more he pays in, the more he can expect to get out. So it is different from taxes in general.

The system would not really make sense if it were just a tax system, because, after all, it is a flat rate of contribution on annual earnings up to a specified ceiling, and that means that it is more burdensome on people with low earnings than on those with higher earnings. Those who earn much more than $7,800, and who are paying the tax just on $7,800, feel it a lot less. As a tax system it is not progressive and not ideal. But it is more than a tax system.

On the other hand, if you look at it as just a benefit system, you would hardly say that it made sense as such, either. This is because it pays out more of its money to better-off people, those who have had higher incomes. Therefore, it pays more money to people who are rich and pays less to people who are poor. So as just a benefit system, it would not make too much sense, either. Nor, of course, would a private pension plan.

Social security makes sense only as a unit—as a tax-and-benefit combination, which we call a social insurance program, where you pay in some money and you get out some money, and the more you have paid in, the more you can expect to get out.

Efficient and Economical

If we no longer had social security, the private pension plans would need to be expanded. And since social security is a relatively inexpensive program, it contributes to an efficient and economical setup for our total economic security arrangement as a whole.

It is administered quite inexpensively. The whole program, with Medicare and with the relatively high administrative costs that that part of the program involves, and also the relatively high administrative costs of the disability program, which involves medical examinations in many cases—the cost overall is about 2 per cent of income, and that includes the check-paying and tax collecting.

INCREASE IN SOCIAL SECURITY TAXES

Social security contributions started out at one per cent of the first $3,000 each for employees and employers, and now they are scheduled, for social security and Medicare combined, to reach a maximum of 5.9 per cent each in the year 1987. This will include 5 per cent for cash benefits, on a base of $7,800 of annual earnings, as against $3,000 in 1937.

Actually, present social insurance contributions of employers, as a percentage of total payroll, turn out to be less, counting both social security and unemployment insurance, than what had been anticipated as the ultimate contribution rate for these two programs together at the time social security was established in 1935. In 1935, the ultimate employer contribution rate was scheduled to be 3 per cent of the first $3,000 of an individual's annual earnings for social security and 3 per cent on total payroll for unemployment insurance.

At that time the $3,000 base covered 92 per cent of total wages, and the ultimate social security contribution represented 2.8 per cent of total payroll. As a percentage of his total payroll, the employer in 1935 could have expected to pay in social security and unemployment insurance contributions an ultimate 5.8 per cent of payroll. After account is taken of the deductibility of the social insurance taxes from income as counted for the purpose of corporation income taxes, the employer's net social security contribution was anticipated ultimately to be 5 per cent of total payroll.

Today, after various expansions of the social security program, the ultimate rate for social security and unemployment insurance (leaving out Medicare) is scheduled to be only 6.2 per cent. The unemployment insurance rate is now about 1.2 per cent of total payroll (as of 1967) as a result of experience rating and of the adoption of a $3,000 contribution base in 1939, which has remained unchanged in federal law and has increased relatively little in most state laws. Also, the social security contribution base has not gone up anywhere nearly in proportion to the increase in payrolls. As a matter of fact, if the ceiling (now $7,800) were to be made comparable with the original ceiling of $3,000 back in 1935, it would be somewhere in the neighborhood of $15,000 to $16,000.

When the federal income tax on corporations is taken into account, the effective rate of social insurance contribution is considerably less than this 6.2 per cent of total payroll would indicate. In fact, when account is taken of the effects of the corporate income tax deductions, the employer's social insurance contribution is less than was anticipated when the ultimate rates were set in 1935. The employer's ultimate net social insurance contribution rate is 3.6 per cent of total payroll when the average corporation tax rate of 42.5 per cent is taken into account.

PROSPECTS FOR FURTHER INCREASES

I ought to say just a word about the future, although I can do so only as a career civil servant. Mr. Nixon and Mr. Humphrey have both made some statements about social security lately—and I am not one to try to get in the middle of that—but let me just say that they have both made proposals for changes in social security, one going somewhat further than the other and one, therefore, involving somewhat more in the way of tax revenue than the other. But both candidates have issued papers that indicate that they mean, at one point or another, to make some changes in social security. In both cases the changes would cost money, which would have to be raised some way.

With Medicare, the now-scheduled ultimate tax rate for social security is well on the way to 6 per cent. It will be 5.9 per cent in 1987.

As the rates go higher, there is naturally more resistance to their being raised further. So I don't think that there is a great deal of room for raising the rates, although they could perhaps be raised to an even 6 per cent. The standards of what people regard as acceptable seem to have changed over the years. It used to be thought, in 1935, that 3 per cent was as high as we could go for social security, and here we are already scheduled to go to 5.9 per cent. So I don't know that you can tell, in any one year, what will be deemed tolerable or acceptable in another year. But I think you cannot go very much higher on the rate.

You could raise the $7,800 ceiling on the amount of earnings taxable and creditable in a year, and there is considerable advantage in raising the ceiling. People who have earnings higher than the present ceiling would get more social security protection. With any given level of benefits, the lower the ceiling is, the higher the tax rate has to be, and the higher the ceiling goes, the lower the rate can be.

I do not believe that Congress is going to raise the ceiling to $15,000 very soon—$15,000 being, roughly, what would be comparable to the 1935 ceiling—but it could be raised some, and there would be some additional income to the system over and above the additional benefit costs that would result. If the ceiling is raised, more benefits will be paid to people who will pay contributions on the higher base, but there is more additional income than additional benefits, so that there is some room for increasing benefits generally.

After an increase in the earnings base ceiling, the only other recourse would be the federal Treasury, and up to now, in the cash benefits part of social security, we have not had any federal contribution. There is a federal contribution for the Medicare part, and there is a payment out of general revenues for a special benefit that was called for in an amendment to the Social Security Act that was enacted in 1966. Under the 1966 provision, persons who reached age 72 before 1968 and who were not insured and had never paid social security contributions might get $40 a month— a payment that comes out of general revenue. It is administered through social security, but it is not part of the social security financing. A federal contribution for the financing of the cash benefits system would be a new departure.

The social security programs in other countries generally do have a government contribution. If there were, by any chance, to be any large-scale increases in benefits, I presume that it would have to come from a general revenue contribution. There are arguments both for and against a government contribution. For lack of time I shall not be able to go into these arguments.

CHAPTER IV

HOW TAXES AFFECT SAVINGS PLANS AND LIFE INSURANCE

Curtis R. Henderson
Vice President, Johnson & Higgins

LET US concentrate today on only two types of benefit plans: savings plans and life insurance. For conclusions regarding tax effects would become even more miscellaneous if applied to more kinds of plans; also, as you will note, there is some relation between savings plans and life insurance.

I. Savings Plans

In the typical savings plan, employees contribute a percentage of pay, which is matched by specified employer contributions and is then invested by the trustee for the employee's account.

Advantages of Qualification under Internal Revenue Code 401 (A)

Most savings plans are qualified under Internal Revenue Code section 401 (a) which affords very substantial federal tax advantages. The most important of these are (a) the ability to invest the employer's contribution without first subjecting it to tax in the employee's own return, and (b) the ability to reinvest investment income without diminution from federal income tax.

Greater Investment Accumulation

Money paid into a qualified plan is deductible by the employer but not taxable to the employee. Thus *all* of the money can be put to work at once. Investment income is exempt from federal income

55

tax, so *all* of it can be reinvested. The interaction of the two factors produces striking results.

Suppose two hypothetical employees, each now 35 years old: George Smith receives a $100-a-year increase in salary; Earl Jones works for a company which pays the $100 for him each year into a qualified plan. In each instance, the available investment produces an investment yield of 5 per cent per year, compounded annually. Assume a top federal tax bracket of 20 per cent throughout, during both active and retirement years.

Here is what happens over the 30-year period remaining until the normal retirement date of each man:

	George Smith	Earl Jones
(a) Additional compensation each year	$ 100 (in pay check)	$ 100 (paid into plan)
(b) Income tax on $100 each year	$ 20	0
(c) Net after-tax amount available for investment	$ 80	$ 100
(d) Effective rate of investment yield on 5 per cent investment	4 per cent	5 per cent
(e) Fund at age 65 accumulated from amount shown in line (c) each year for 30 years at the rate shown in line (d)	$4,487	$6,644
(f) Annual income provided by the lump-sum amount shown in line (e)	$ 374	$ 554
(g) Income tax each year on the amount shown in line (f)	$ 15	$ 111
(h) Net after-tax income each year during retirement	$ 359	$ 443

The $15 that Smith pays in income tax is a 20 per cent· tax on $75, which is the *excess* of annuity over $299, the amount he receives tax-free under the annuity rules on account of his $4,487 "investment in the contract," (as it is referred to in Internal Revenue Code section 72.) Jones' income tax payment is a 20 per cent tax on the *whole* annuity payment.

This is a conservative illustration. It assumes investment income of only 5 per cent. If the fund had earned 8 per cent, the $6,644 shown for Jones in line (e) would have been $11,328. Also, the assumption is a tax bracket of only 20 per cent, which remains the same during active and retirement years. In real life, Jones (for whom the $100 was paid into the plan) would be in a lower tax bracket during retirement years; and he and his wife would each have an additional $600 federal income tax exemption when 65.

Earl Jones would have two additional advantages not reflected in the foregoing comparison:

1. No tax is payable when the trustee realizes gain in order to shift to another investment, and

2. The annuity rates at which the trustee buys Jones' annuity will be more favorable than rates available to Jones (because of wholesale purchasing power and the favorable federal income tax treatment that is given insurance companies with respect to the funds they hold on account of annuities sold to trustees of qualified plans.)

Other Advantages

When the whole fund is distributed in a lump sum following retirement, there will be:

1. Long-term capital gain rates, which are half the ordinary rates with a maximum rate of 25 per cent, and

2. A special exemption for employer stock distributed in kind at retirement or death—no tax at all on the amount by which the stock increased in value while held in trust. (If the retired employee holds the stock until he dies, his beneficiary takes value at his death as tax cost for later sale, so that the value which escaped tax at retirement will *never* be subject to federal income tax.)

Distribution Following Death

If an employee dies either before or after retirement, any part of the funds held for him which is distributed to a beneficiary other than his estate and which is *not* attributable to his own contributions is fully exempt from the federal *estate* tax without any dollar limit.

On lump-sum distributions following death *after retirement,* the beneficiaries will also have available for income tax purposes the long-term capital gain treatment and special exemption for employer stock described above.

CHOICE BETWEEN PENSION AND PROFIT-SHARING

One choice an employee must make in connection with a savings plan qualified under IRC section 401 (a) is whether to select a "pension" or a "profit-sharing" plan. Pension and profit-sharing plans have very different shapes in common practice; but when it gets down to what you can do or cannot do within the framework of section 401, there are only these differences:

1. In a pension plan but not a profit-sharing plan, you can give substantial credit for prior service, and you can allocate current service money in favor of older employees.

2. In a profit-sharing plan, but not a pension plan, you can allocate forfeitures among participants, and you can permit participants who are still employed to withdraw credits attributable to employer contributions.

Looking at these differences, most employers qualify their savings plans as "profit-sharing" plans. This can be done very simply without getting involved with contributions that fluctuate with profits. You just make the formal text of the plan provide that employer contributions will be made only from current income or accumulated earnings. This is a sort of magic phrase inserted to put the critical label, "profit-sharing plan," on the Internal Revenue Service's copy of your savings plan.

While it may come as a surprise to some laymen, "accumulated earnings" is not an accountant's phrase. It comes from Internal Revenue Code 316 defining the corporate distributions which are taxable as dividends. Some of you will recall, in connection with the World War II excess profits tax, how few experts at the time could tell a corporation what its accumulated earnings really were. As a practical matter, it is not likely that this will become an urgent question in the operation of your savings plan as a profit-sharing plan.

Choice of Payment Options at Retirement

Now let us look at an employee's choice of payment options at time of retirement. Let me urge that you give participants in your savings plan the background knowledge which will prevent a participant who is retiring from automatically reaching for a lump-sum, long-term capital gains distribution, unless that is truly the best choice for him.

The all too common practice in case of a highly-paid retiring executive is to use an annuity illustration, showing him how much larger his after-tax income will be if he takes a lump-sum distribution, pays the 25 per cent long-term capital gains tax, and uses the remaining 75 per cent to purchase an annuity—thus providing a substantial "investment in the contract" (as they call it in Internal Revenue Code section 72) so that a large part of each year's annuity payment will come back to him tax-free.

The fault in this approach is that it fails to recognize what a bourgeois device an annuity is. Only middle-bracket people are interested in it. The well-to-do individual can live on investment income. He does not need the relatively small increase in current income made possible by the annuity principle. He is probably far more interested in creating the maximum possible estate for his beneficiaries.

Disadvantages of Lump-Sum Payment for Highly-Paid Executives

For such a well-to-do individual, lump-sum payment which he uses to purchase an annuity is not likely to provide the best results. For him, lump-sum payment has these disadvantages:

1. A very substantial part of his account—one-fourth of it—goes for federal income taxes at the beginning of his retirement years, thus depriving his beneficiaries of investment income that otherwise he might accumulate on this money during what we hope will be a long and happy period.

2. The whole fund is also taken out of the federal *estate* tax exemption given to qualified plans.

3. The whole fund is also taken out of the federal *income* tax shelter given to qualified plans, so that gains realized in shifting from one investment to another are subject to capital gains tax—a marked disadvantage compared with the tax-sheltered fund in which investment managers can shift investments at will without being concerned about the taxes thereby incurred.

A series of installments over, say, 20 years is likely to be better for the highly-paid executive than lump-sum distribution. (We are talking here about installment liquidation of units, so he keeps an equity position in the undistributed balance.) The following illustration shows how installment payments can be better than lump-sum payment.

Where the Objective is Creating the Largest Possible Estate.
Suppose a participant in a noncontributory savings or profit-sharing plan retires at age 65. He has $1 million in the fund (100,000 units, each with a value of $10.) The investment income available during post-retirement years is 8 per cent. The plan uses unit accounting, with reinvested dividends reflected in the dollar value of the unit.

If the employee chooses *lump-sum distribution,* he receives $1 million subject to long-term capital gains tax of $250,000 paid to the government at the beginning of his retirement years. The 8 per cent yield on the balance of $750,000 will provide an annual income of $60,000 subject to ordinary income tax rates.

On the death of the employee, the $750,000, together with any unspent accumulation, will go to his beneficiaries free of income tax but subject to federal estate tax. An employee for whom $1 million had been accumulated in the savings plan would be likely to have other assets which would push this $750,000 into a high federal estate tax bracket.

If the employee, on the other hand, chooses *20-year liquidation,* 5 per cent of his units (i.e., 5,000 units) will be cancelled in the first year, and for these he will receive $50,000 subject to tax at ordinary income tax rates. In the fifteenth year, when the unit value has increased (at 8 per cent per year) to $29.37, the value of the 5,000 units distributed in that year will be $146,850.

If the employee should die immediately after retirement and before any distribution is made, the whole $1 million will go to his beneficiaries free from federal estate tax (assuming that none of it was payable to his estate) but subject to long-term capital gains tax. If he had spread this among a number of grandchildren who had no other net income, the tax to them at long-term capital gain rates could easily have been as low as 8 or 10 per cent. (In this example, the currently applicable 10 per cent surtax is ignored.)

If the employee should die in the fifteenth year of retirement, 25,000 units would still stand to his credit, at a unit value of $29.37, making a total value of $743,250, which would go to his beneficiaries wholly exempt from federal estate tax and subject only to long-term capital gains tax computed separately for each beneficiary.

Disadvantages of Lump-Sum Payment for Middle-Bracket Executives

Lump-sum payment is not the best choice for the individual who is in a middle income tax bracket either. He will get more after-tax retirement income if the trustee buys an annuity for him than if he takes a lump sum and buys the annuity, himself.

Where the Objective is Maximum Retirement Income. For instance, let us look at a middle-bracket employee who reaches age 65 and who is a participant in a noncontributory savings or profit-sharing plan in which $100,000 has been accumulated for him. Suppose his wife is the same age as he, and he has no other income or deductions. Assume that he can buy a life annuity at a premium of $12 for each $1 of lifetime annual income, but that the rates available to the trustee enable the trustee to buy $1 of lifetime annual income for men of 65 for only $11. Here is a comparison, based on 1967 federal income tax rates and the standard deduction (ignoring the 10 per cent surtax), between (1) lump-sum distribution and purchase of an annuity by the employee, and (2) purchase of an annuity by the trustee.

The results of acceptance by the employee of a lump sum of $100,000 at the time of retirement, which he uses to purchase an annuity of that amount for himself, would be:

Long-term capital gain tax paid *at beginning* of retirement years	$15,360
Net available for annuity purchase	$84,640
Annuity @ $12	$ 7,053
Federal income tax each year	0
Net annual retirement income	$ 7,053

Note that because of the "annuity exclusion" attributable to the $84,640 purchase price of his annuity, only $1,410 out of the $7,053 is taxable. This is more than covered by the exemptions of $2,400 and the standard deduction of $141 (10 per cent of taxable income). Thus, during *each year of retirement* the employee wastes a large part of his exemptions and a large part of the $1,000 limit on the 10 per cent standard deduction.

If, on the other hand, the trustee purchases a $100,000 annuity for the employee, the results would be:

Annuity	$9,091
Federal income tax each year	$ 959
Net annual retirement income	$8,132

In this case, the employee has no annuity exclusion; the whole $9,091 is subject to tax. However, he makes full use of his $2,400 exemptions for *each year of retirement,* and his standard deduction is $909 for *each year of retirement.*

An important factor to an executive deciding between lump-sum payment and installment payment at time of retirement is that, if he takes installment payments and dies before they are completed, the balance can go to his beneficiaries in a lump sum with all the tax advantages that were available to the employee himself at retirement.

II. LIFE INSURANCE

The most important tax advantage of life insurance—death benefits exempt from federal income taxes—is not peculiar to employee plans. It is provided in Internal Revenue Code section 101 for all life insurance policies, whether individual or group insurance.

Tax Advantage of Group Term Insurance

Group term insurance does have one tax advantage for employees which is not available to individual policyholders: the employee is not taxed either on the premium paid for him by the employer or on the value of the life insurance protection he enjoys.

This particular tax advantage, however, was somewhat impaired by Internal Revenue Code section 79, enacted in 1966, which makes employees taxable on the imputed value of group term life insurance in excess of $50,000. The tax is relatively light, because the table of imputed values used by the Internal Revenue Service is quite low; but the administrative burden imposed on the employer in determining and reporting this imputed value can be a nuisance.

In any event, we should not let this small erosion of the tax benefit for employee group life insurance take our attention away from the main tax advantage—complete tax exemption for the death proceeds. This advantage is still available and is probably fairly secure against legislative attack, because it is available to all life insurance, whether or not employee insurance.

An application of this important tax advantage for life insurance which should have more attention today is in providing survivor benefits during an employee's active years. Survivor income group life insurance has an advantage over such benefits paid from a pension plan, because the death proceeds are fully exempt from income tax.[1]

A typical survivor benefit plan might provide, say, 20 per cent of the pay of an employee until what would have been his sixty-fifth birthday, with perhaps a reduced amount continuing thereafter for the life of a surviving spouse. Such an insurance plan has two advantages over the more conventional group life plans which typically provide a multiple of annual pay for all employees regardless of age:

1. Survivor income group life insurance automatically fits the amount of insurance more closely to the need—providing a large amount of insurance for the younger employee whose death deprives his family of the larger number of future pay checks.

2. The cost picture is more manageable because in survivor group life insurance the amount of insurance automatically decreases as the cost of insurance increases with the employee's age.

Another Pattern Suggested

Now, changing the subject, let me suggest another possible pattern for employee life insurance. Unlike the survivor group life insurance just discussed, this one is, so far, only a theoretical pattern which I think might have practical application in some specialized situations:

1. As an employee-pay-all supplement to a noncontributory group life insurance plan, when the employer would like to pro-

---

[1] Some higher paid employees may prefer the survivor benefit paid from the pension plan, because it can clearly be made exempt from federal estate tax.

vide a wider range of choice as to the amount of insurance that is feasible in group plans;

2. As an employee-pay-all group life plan for the employer who provides no employer-supported group insurance for his employees; or

3. As an employee-pay-all supplement to a savings plan or other employer-sponsored investment program for employees.

The suggestion here is simply that we work out an individual life insurance policy so drastically simplified that it will achieve many of the economies and ease of administration that we have in group life insurance, without being subject to the disadvantages of group insurance. Such a special individual policy would be very different from conventional individual policies, in that it would have absolutely no long-range guarantees as to annuity options or interest paid on installment payouts. Commissions would be so low that the policy would have practical application only for payroll deduction or other mass enrollment situations.

This special individual policy would also differ from group insurance. It would not reflect mortality restricted to the employer's own group of employees. This point might actually be an advantage. Life insurance claim experience is not subject to the same possibilities of abuse as hospitalization or disability insurance; and an employer could accept with equanimity in life insurance the idea that the experience will not be limited to his own group of employees. Actually, the life insurance industry itself might be happier to see mortality thrown into a larger pool. The industry has experienced a number of instances in which a large claim in a small group case led the employer simply to cancel the group contract and start again with a new life insurance company.

Let me suggest a specific pattern for this specially designed individual life insurance policy: The policy for each employee would specify the premium he pays; and the amount of insurance provided would be stated as a multiple of monthly premium depending on attained age at time of death. If we were to use a table based on, say, 120 per cent of the 1958 CSO mortality table, the amount of insurance would be 5,300 times the monthly premium for a man who dies at age 22, or 400 times for a man who dies at age 64. Thus, a man paying a premium of $10 a month would have $53,000 of insurance at age 22, or $4,000 at age 64. Rates for each year of age between 21 and 64 are shown in the accompanying table.

SPECIAL INDIVIDUAL DECREASING TERM LIFE INSURANCE POLICIES
SCHEDULE OF LIFE INSURANCE

Attained Age When Death Occurs	Amount of Insurance as Multiple of Monthly Premium	Attained Age When Death Occurs	Amount of Insurance as Multiple of Monthly Premium
21 or younger	$5,600	43	$2,200
22	5,300	44	2,000
23	5,300	45	1,900
24	5,300	46	1,700
25	5,300	47	1,600
26	5,000	48	1,500
27	5,000	49	1,400
28	5,000	50	1,300
29	4,800	51	1,200
30	4,800	52	1,100
31	4,500	53	1,000
32	4,300	54	900
33	4,300	55	800
34	4,200	56	800
35	4,000	57	700
36	3,800	58	600
37	3,600	59	600
38	3,300	60	500
39	3,000	61	500
40	2,800	62	400
41	2,600	63	400
42	2,400	64	400

Note: This schedule means, for example, that if an individual pays a monthly premium of $10, his life insurance will be $53,000 if he dies at age 22, or $4,000 if he dies at age 63.

With these individual policies, each employee would be paying the full cost of his insurance at his current age. The rate basis I have used for illustrative purposes would mean that an employee under age 26 would be paying less than 20 cents per month per $1,000; and an employee 64 years of age would be paying $2.50 per month per $1,000. These insurance policies would be participating, so that the employees could reasonably expect to enjoy experience dividends.

Like other individual policies, these would require that each prospective insured person furnish proof of insurability. In many cases a simple health statement from the individual would be enough. In other cases the insurance company would ask for a medical examination.

These drastically simplified individual policies happen automatically to provide decreasing term insurance, which makes them an ideal complement for the investment accumulation building up in a savings plan. For the employee who does not want his insurance to decrease quite so fast, we could provide that he could make regular increases, say, 6 per cent per year, in his monthly premium, and thus the amount of his insurance, without furnishing further evidence of insurability.

With such a program an employer could indulge his employees in the widest range of selection as to amount of insurance; and he could do it without being in the least concerned as to how many of them sign up, or for what amounts.[2]

---

[2] Author's Note, June, 1969: "This new type of individual insurance policy presented in this paper as a 'theoretical pattern' has been adopted by two insurance companies and is now coming onto the market."

CHAPTER V

VARIABLE ANNUITIES AND PENSION PLANNING

Kenneth C. Foster
Executive Vice President,
The Prudential Insurance Company of America

EARLIER this week you may have seen in the newspaper that United States Senator H. A. Williams, Jr. of New Jersey introduced a bill to establish an Institute of Retirement Income, which would recommend improvements in programs for the elderly, including social security, private pensions, and other forms of old-age assistance. The Senator termed "income maintenance" the principal problem facing elderly persons, and went on to say:

> If older Americans are forced to exist on inadequate incomes, far below the standard of younger men and women, they are not going to be able to take advantage of any program of social progress or community service.[1]

Recent issues of *Fortune* have carried a series of articles on changing industries, and the current issue contains one entitled "Life Insurance's Almighty Leap Into Equities." That article begins as follows:

> Nowhere in the whole panoply of changing American business are changes of a more fundamental and repercussive character brewing than in that citadel of conservatism, the U.S. life-insurance industry. What's happening here might be regarded, in almost any other business, as a modest move into product diversification. But this is the life-insurance industry—historically the champion of the stable dollar, the foe of inflation, the scourge of speculation. And it's going to start selling common stocks.[2]

---

[1] *Congressional Record*, October 1, 1968, S.11814 (introduction of S.4115).
[2] *Fortune*, October, 1968, p. 142.

INSURANCE INDUSTRY IS FOE OF INFLATION

I think I can speak for all of us in the industry when I say that we are still the foe of inflation, we are still for the stable dollar, and we are not about to sell common stocks in any literal sense. But most—not all—of us have come to recognize the fact that there are changes in the economic climate that make it advisable to balance our traditional contracts, based largely on fixed dollar obligations and fixed dollar investments, with contracts related to equities.

Senator Williams' statement points out one problem, and the article in *Fortune* points out a solution in the direction of equities. Let us see how those two things tie together and where variable annuities fit into the picture. Here are some of the well-known facts, with assumptions and ideas that most people have today:

1. From 1940 to 1950, increased prices decreased purchasing power by nearly 50 per cent. From 1950 to 1967, increased prices decreased purchasing power by nearly 30 per cent. Price increases in 1968 are not reassuring—and that certainly is an understatement. One speaker has referred to it as a 4 per cent inflationary rate. Some significant increase in the cost of living will probably continue over the years ahead—that also is an understatement. Some significant increase in the standard of living will probably continue in the years ahead—that is probably an understatement.

2. People are retiring earlier, which means more years in retirement. People are living longer, which means even more years in retirement. If you add 15 years or so of retirement pay-out to 35 or 40 years of thrifty pay-in, this adds up to a long period for eroding forces to do their work. And, of course, none would forget federal income taxes, state income taxes, estate taxes, inheritance taxes, real estate taxes, sales taxes, and numerous other taxes—direct and indirect, obvious and hidden—which tend to increase with remarkable persistence.

3. To top it off, people are no longer satisfied to live on the edge of life. People feel today that they are entitled to what they regard as their fair share of the economic and social goods that we produce.

Now, in these times of changing values, monetary and otherwise, it is little wonder that annuities have become variable, too.

When Mr. David spoke about the social security system, you will note that he had unique justification for the periodic increases in social security payments. Most people would consider social security payments as fixed-dollar in nature, but actually, since they "increase" every couple of years, perhaps they are variable in nature. At least they are changing in nature and do attempt to keep up with the increased cost of living and the increased standard of living.

The history of insurance company operations, world-wide, indicates several early searches for "indexed" contracts. Generally, these were devised as a means for avoiding the effects of currency inflation. For example, in Germany, in the mid-twenties, some insurance companies experimented with contracts that were linked to the price of specific commodities such as wheat. As early as 1929, a courageous American investment counselor suggested that insurance companies should pay more attention to purchasing power, rather than just dollars, and should invest more money in common stocks. The British life insurance companies have traditionally invested much more of their assets in common stocks than have the American companies.

COLLEGE RETIREMENT EQUITIES FUND

The modern era of variable annuities commenced with the College Retirement Equities Fund (CREF) of the Teachers Insurance and Annuity Association (TIAA). It is a long and well-documented story, which I shall not attempt to go into in detail. The report that was made by the TIAA research people, however, led to a great deal of thinking that there must be a better way of providing annuities for college professors and for employees of colleges and certain nonprofit or exempt institutions. As a result of that thinking and studies that were done in connection with it, TIAA came to the conclusion that the best solution was a combination of fixed dollar and equity base. The particular technical breakthrough of the TIAA study was the development of a lifetime income which would vary in dollar amount to reflect the investment results of a portfolio invested in common stocks.

This organization was started in New York in 1952, and by the end of 1967, CREF covered more than 200,000 individuals, and had accumulated assets in excess of $950 million. Originally,

CREF permitted an individual, typically a college professor, to invest up to 50 per cent in equities, with the balance in fixed dollar investments. More recently, the equity maximum has been increased to 75 per cent.

Results of CREF have been impressive and provide the one large body of experience with some maturity. A unit value of $10 in the annuity year 1952-53 has shown a rewarding increase, with only occasional temporary setbacks, to a current value of $29.90.

Of course, this idea began to spread to other groups. Among the first to recognize its significance were airline pilots. Airline pilots, as you know, retire at relatively young ages and have to look forward to a rather long period of retirement. As a result, they were particularly interested in the effects of inflation.

INTEREST IN EQUITIES

As the influences of the great depression wore off and a new generation began making decisions in a new economic climate after World War II, there was general interest in equities to fund pensions. Some employers with trusteed or self-administered plans providing fixed dollar benefits invested pension reserves in common stocks, expecting that increased return, including appreciation, would reduce their costs. The employer took the risk of loss but also had the opportunity for gain. The employee's fixed dollar benefits were not directly affected one way or the other by the investment experience—except that favorable experience put the employers in a better position to afford to liberalize benefits.

Insurance companies interested in pensions began to see the effects of the development of interest, both in equities and in variable annuities. Prudential, for example, started its studies more than 15 years ago. It has been a long, messy road—too long to describe here.

VARIABLE ANNUITY BENEFITS

In order to provide variable annuity benefits, an insurance company segregates amounts received by it, under such contracts, from its other assets, and invests them in a diversified portfolio of common stocks held in a separate account. Upon retirement, the holder of a variable annuity receives a monthly income for life, just as under a fixed dollar annuity. The essential difference is that payments under a variable annuity change from month to month to reflect investment results, including market value changes, of the common stock portfolio.

As the annuitant stands to gain from increases in value, he also bears the risk of decreases. Although the insurance company does not and cannot guarantee the dollar amount of the monthly annuity payments, which depend on the investment performance of this portfolio, it does guarantee that the annuity payments will be made for the lifetime of the annuitant and that the dollar amounts of the payments will be unaffected by how long he, or anyone else, lives.

With all the obstacles that slowed the start of separate accounts by insurance companies in this country, the growth of separate-account assets is impressive. It was 1962 before law and regulation allowed us to set up a separate account, and this was used initially only for group equity funding, where the results of the investment in common stocks directly affected only the employer's cost, but *not* the employee's benefits. It was 1964 before we could write our first group variable annuity contract. But by the end of 1967, the total assets held in the separate accounts of all United States life insurance companies was $1.2 billion.

PRUDENTIAL EXPERIENCE

Prudential's experience with equity investments has taken place over about the same period as CREF has been in operation.

1. In the general account of our company, in which we hold the reserves for our fixed dollar contracts, we have been investing in equities since 1950. At the end of 1967, our equity portfolio in this account exceeded a billion dollars.

2. In our separate account, which started in 1962, we had more than 130 participating group contracts at the end of 1967, representing over $400 million in market value. By the end of 1968, we expect to have more than 200 group contracts participating in our separate accounts, representing over $800 million in assets.

We feel that variable annuities are now established as a means of enabling retired people to maintain real income, which I think is what Senator Williams meant, in the face of increasing cost of living and the increasing standard of living. In the variable annuity plan for Prudential employees, the unit value which started at $10 in December, 1962, reached $16.26 by January, 1968.

Professor Holland has referred to state and local pension funds as the sleeping giants in a growth industry. These funds have recently shown considerable interest in variable annuities. Unions have also shown considerable interest and some action in variable annuities recently. Employers are interested, of course, although there is always the question of who is going to pay for what.

Variable annuities are by no means recommended by all pension planners for all situations. Some feel, for example, that variable annuities may be appropriate for conversion at retirement, for profit-sharing plans, or for money-purchase type plans, but question their broader application. The thought can be expressed, on the one hand, that, if the plan is very successful, the retired employee would be paid too much, or, looking at it from a more practical direction, that the employer is paying too much for his pension plan.

Variable annuity benefits, however, as a companion to fixed dollar benefits in building a total pension plan seem to be appreciated and understood by rank and file employees, not just by the more sophisticated college professors. Our experience on many cases indicates a very high degree of acceptance. When we gave a choice to our own employees, including our insurance agents, more than 98 per cent chose the balanced plan including variable annuity benefits. This is quite typical, to find more than 90 per cent in favor of the variable annuity when the choice is given.

The life insurance industry now has in full operation equity funding facilities as well as facilities for providing variable benefits on a group basis. We still have some impediments. We cannot accept employee contributions on a variable basis under qualified pension plans. We regard this as inequitable treatment under law and regulation, compared with a trusteed plan. We have achieved equality in most areas. We are hopeful that we shall soon have it in this area also.

INDIVIDUAL VARIABLE ANNUITIES

I have said nothing about individual contracts of variable annuities. The principles are exactly the same as in group, of course, and the reason I have not mentioned them is that our company is in a delicate position at the moment. We have things pending about which we are not permitted to talk in public. One certainly can say that individual variable annuities are developing very rapidly. We think they will become important in pension planning and probably particularly important as supplements in pension planning.

The type of thinking that Mr. Henderson expressed in reference to individual policies of life insurance as a supplement in employee benefit plans[3] can probably be applied in the next few years to individual variable annuity policies as well. They may be even more important as a supplement to pension funding.

Although I assume all the facts that I have presented to be tentative and the concepts to be temporary, I recommend that in pension planning situations you give most serious consideration to the potential use of a variable annuity, either during the accumulation period or during the payout period, or both. They have great strength and some weaknesses; they fit many situations, but not all situations. They should not be ignored. And you should, of course, remember what we are fond of saying in Prudential, "The future belongs to those who prepare for it."

---

[3] See end of Chapter 4 of this volume.

CHAPTER VI

PROPOSALS FOR MINIMIZING INSURANCE PREMIUM TAXES ON WELFARE BENEFITS FOR EMPLOYEES

LLOYD E. SLATER

Deputy Commissioner for Tax Research,
New York State Department of Taxation and Finance

WHEN the program for this symposium was under discussion, I suggested that this topic, which can be dealt with here only in a brief way, was important enough to occupy a full panel session at this symposium. Even then, the risks in making such a suggestion were obvious, since I might be tabbed as chairman of the panel. In that event, though, I had envisioned that it would be possible to call on speakers representing several competing points of view. I had studied insurance taxes for more than six years, and—while I hadn't found many answers—it seemed that perhaps I knew enough about the problem areas to be an antagonist and stir up controversy.

A Controversial Topic

I may still stir up just as much, or more, controversy. It is doubtful that this subject can be treated in an impartial way, and some of you may be unhappy about the way I treat it. Unfortunately, you will not have a full opportunity for rebuttal, but there will hopefully be some time for questions and comments.

In the time available I shall review a few of the important features of state taxes on insurance; enumerate and comment briefly on some of the ways that have been employed, and are now being tried, to reduce these taxes; and mention some of the measures the state of New York is considering in order to protect state revenue.

STATE PREMIUM TAXES

The common state taxes on insurance—usually applying only to the nonpension portion of insured employee welfare benefits—are based on premiums. The typical tax rates are from 2 per cent to 2¼ per cent. While annuity considerations are mostly exempt from tax, this is not true in all of the states. It does happen to be true in New York.

In spite of the simplicity of the above statement, state taxes on insurance are characterized by a remarkable absence of uniformity. We currently hear much discussion about the lack of uniformity in other areas of state taxation, but those differences are minor in comparison with what we find in insurance taxation.

Our New York State Tax Structure Study Committee began a study of the taxation of insurance in 1962. It was soon apparent that the problems of group insurance, which we are discussing this morning, are closely tied to many other problems inherent in the present system of state insurance taxation. We have now been bogged down in this morass of problems for more than six years, and only a few of the unique features of insurance taxes can be covered here.

Although every state imposes some form of tax on insurance premiums, many states also tax some portion of the industry on some other basis. Furthermore, even in those states which may at first appear to have a similar tax base, due to differences in tax rate, deductions or exemptions, the effect of their taxes may be quite different. Some states also have alternative or supplemental taxes, and then there is that oddity in the insurance tax field— discriminatory and retaliatory taxation.

DISCRIMINATION AND RETALIATION

This oddity in insurance taxation, which is of particular importance in the group insurance field, exists today because for many years the Supreme Court ruled that the business of insurance was not interstate commerce, and, therefore, was not subject to any administration, supervision, or limitation, by the federal government. When the Court finally began to change its mind in this area, the Congress enacted what is known as the McCarran Act

—which has made it possible for one-half of the states to continue their former practice of openly and intentionally placing a higher rate of tax on insurance purchased from an out-of-state company than on insurance purchased from a company within the state.

In addition to the half of the states that wilfully discriminate against all out-of-state insurance companies, there are a number of states which, ostensibly in self-defense, impose a higher rate of tax only on companies from any state that charges the companies of the first state a higher tax than the first state would otherwise have charged. This retaliation is based on the barbaric concept that: "Whatever you do to my companies, I will do to your companies."

An Incentive for Tax Avoidance

Before leaving this brief analysis of state taxes on insurance, let me emphasize that important effects result from the amount of state tax that is levied. As previously explained, the typical tax is on premiums, and the typical rate is 2 per cent to $2\frac{1}{4}$ per cent—which is a low percentage. On the other hand, this rate is applied to what can be a very high base, and the total tax on a large group insurance policy is sufficiently important to have encouraged many people to explore ways of avoiding this expense. In fact, some of the best brains in this country are being devoted to this essentially nonproductive activity.

Industry representatives, in trying to emphasize the size of their state tax bills, have pointed out that in some instances the tax payment can be as much as 40 per cent of the loading cost—not including actual claims—in insuring and administering employee benefit plans. Although that statement probably magnifies too much the importance of state insurance taxes, these taxes have been sufficiently important to encourage strenuous efforts to eliminate them, or get around them.

Premium Taxes on Group Insurance Are Also Important to the States

I should also point out the importance of these taxes to the states. In New York we are now collecting in the neighborhood of $25 million each year in premium taxes on group insurance, and throughout all the states it has been estimated that the total yield of these taxes is as much as $200 million per year. While these are not tremendous amounts of money in relation to total state budgets, even these amounts of revenue would be very difficult to replace in our present situation, where the states must continually find new ways to finance the demands for expanded services.

TAX-EXEMPT COMPETITION

Turning now to the methods that have been used in trying to get around, or minimize, state taxes on employee welfare benefits, the first is coverage of these benefits in hospital service and medical and dental group plans, such as Blue Cross. As a layman I do not fully appreciate the viewpoint that a Blue Cross contract is not "insurance," while a policy issued by an insurance company is "insurance." Because of that distinction, and for a variety of other reasons, many states have exempted from their premium taxes the charges made by hospital service, medical, and dental groups. Thus, insurance companies face a tax disadvantage in this rather large area.

The studies we have made in New York indicate that this cannot have been an insurmountable handicap in recent years, because hospital service, medical and dental plans have not grown any faster than insurance plans. Even so, insured plans might have grown much faster without this handicap, and this is one of the ways that has been employed to avoid premium taxes.

"SELF-INSURANCE"

Another tax avoidance method is what is called—incorrectly—self-insurance: actually it is more accurate to call it noninsurance. Employee benefits are provided by the employer, rather than obtained from an insurance company. This is not self-insurance, because self-insurance occurs only when an individual, having a risk that does not involve any other party, decides not to insure, but to accept and absorb the losses from that risk.

An employer who goes into what is called self-insurance is not in that situation, since he agrees to provide benefits to employees, who are separate entities. Under the laws of many states, such an employer has actually entered into the insurance business and

77

may be subject to premium taxes. In the past, though, such employers have mostly avoided these taxes.

DOMESTIC INSURERS VS. OUT-OF-STATE INSURERS

Another possibility for reducing the amount of state taxes on employee benefit plans is to pick an insurance company that will be favored so far as taxes are concerned. As previously mentioned, more than one-half the states discriminate and impose a higher tax on some insurance companies than on others.

One example of such discrimination sparked a new effort at tax avoidance called the Met-Cat plan. This was a policy written by the Metropolitan Life Insurance Company for the Caterpillar Tractor Company. Metropolitan had been insuring Caterpillar employees under a group plan and there was considerable pressure to find a way to reduce premium taxes. The employer may have threatened to go to self-insurance, but this is not substantiated. In any event, the employer did not have to self-insure to avoid much of the tax incurred under the Metropolitan plan. Caterpillar has most of its employees in the state of Illinois, which exempts premiums paid to one of its domestic insured companies, while collecting the full tax on premiums paid to a foreign insurance company.

Thus Metropolitan was at a tax disadvantage, and faced possible loss of this business either to "self-insurance" or to an Illinois insurance company. This was not a unique situation, since New York insurance companies face the same kind of disadvantage in about one-half of the states. In this instance, however, Metropolitan developed a new type of insurance policy in an effort to avoid premium taxes, and that development will be discussed later.

A TAX LOOPHOLE

Another tax avoidance method that has been tried by some—I don't know how successfully, and it certainly rests on weak ground—involves a loophole in our tax laws and a Supreme Court decision relating to the Connecticut General Life Insurance Company.[1] This loophole makes it possible to avoid premium taxes

---

[1] Connecticut General Life Ins. Co. v. Johnson, 303 U.S. 77, 82 L. ed. 676 (1937).

when an insurance policy can somehow be placed with a company that is not admitted to do business in New York. Such a transaction would be conducted outside the state and there is no way for New York to tax it under our present tax laws.

The servicing of such a policy would probably be unsatisfactory, if the Supreme Court had not ruled that an insurance policy —once it is written—can be reinsured with a foreign insurance company without becoming taxable: it would be taxable if reinsured with a domestic insurance company. Thus, if a policy written by a nonadmitted carrier is reinsured with a foreign company admitted to do business in New York, it may be possible to avoid entirely New York's insurance premium taxes and still provide satisfactory service on the contract.

We do not know how extensive this type of avoidance may be and I do not like to publicize it. I do so only because we feel confident that we shall find a way to plug this loophole, and, in any event, it is a part of the overall picture. We are also very much concerned about this tax loophole and I shall refer to it again later.

MET-CAT; NOW EVOLVED TO MINI-MET

I shall discuss only one more method that is being used in attempts to reduce premium taxes on group insurance. This is the Met-Cat type of policy, already alluded to, which was developed by the Metropolitan Life Insurance Company in conjunction with the Caterpillar Tractor Company. This type of policy has now gone through an extended period of evolution in which it has been designated by various names, with the most recent being Mini-Met plan. This plan seemingly attempts to transfer legally from the insurance company to the employer a major portion of responsibility, without actually doing so. Thus, the employer is represented as directly paying most claims, and it is argued that the only "premium" paid to Metropolitan covers loading charges plus a small cushion or reserve—a small cushion is ample for health-type benefits. Actually, the employer usually sets up a special bank account on which the insurance company draws claim checks, and this replaces most of the former premium.

The objective of this plan is to reduce the premium tax to approximately 10 per cent of what it would have been under conventional group insurance policies.

HARMFUL EFFECTS OF TAX AVOIDANCE

If the current efforts to avoid premium taxes on group insurance are successful, New York will lose potentially $20 million of premium tax annually, and other states will lose a substantial amount of revenue. There is also great danger that the quality of employee welfare benefits would be seriously impaired. Particularly as employers go the route of so-called—but misnamed—noninsurance or self-insurance, more supervision would be required to assure that the benefits, when received, will actually be what was presented and expected.

There are also important implications for the insurance industry itself. Without trying to represent the industry and its points

PERCENTAGE OF INSURANCE HANDLED BY NEW YORK COMPANIES

Type of Insurance	Individual Policies		Group Policies	
	1950	1965	1950	1965
Risks Located in New York:				
Life insurance	43.6%	45.7%	51.9%	49.5%
Accident & health insurance	27.7	35.8[a]	40.6	37.0[a]
Total Risks in United States:				
Life insurance	30.4	28.7	56.3	30.6
Accident & health insurance		Not available	29.2	22.9

[a] Information shown is for 1964, instead of 1965.
Source: Unpublished material assembled by the New York State Tax Structure Study Committee.

of view, I can report that there are strong feelings within the industry that acceptance of the "minimum premium" or Mini-Met plan would be a harmful development. To the extent that legal responsibilities are actually shifted, the implications for the industry may be very dangerous.

At the same time, the existence of other tax avoidance schemes has had a serious effect on insurance companies in New York, and they have not been holding their share of group insurance business.

Information showing changes in the percentage of insurance handled by New York companies, which has been assembled by the New York State Tax Structure Study Committee, is shown in the accompanying table. This reveals that from 1950 to 1965 New York insurance companies actually increased their percentage of the New York market for individual policies both in the life insurance and health insurance fields. However, during the same period they lost ground in the group insurance area.

In the United States as a whole, the share of the group insurance market handled by New York domestic companies showed a more drastic decline, with their percentage of group life insurance dropping from 56.3 per cent in 1950 to 30.6 per cent in 1965, and their percentage of group accident and health insurance going from 29.2 per cent in 1950 to 22.9 per cent in 1965.

Possible Actions in New York

To round out the current situation in New York relative to premium tax avoidance, I shall enumerate briefly a few possible actions that are currently under consideration.

1. There is a possibility that hospitalization and medical payments types of insurance will be made fully tax-exempt, which would eliminate the tax inequity between insurance and Blue Cross types of coverage. This was proposed in a bill sponsored by the Administration last year. That bill would also have required employers to provide certain insurance for employees, and it failed because there was opposition to that part of the bill. Thus, there is a possibility of complete tax exemption on the Blue Cross/Blue Shield types of coverage, even when supplied by an insurance company.

2. It also seems likely that there will be increased efforts on the part of New York to make more effective the taxes that will remain on other types of group insurance.

3. The attorney general is being asked for an opinion, to supplement one obtained earlier, in relation to the Mini-Met plan. Consideration is also being given to the possibility that, if an insurance company is ruled exempt from a portion of the premium tax, the employer involved may have become an insurance company—by taking over obligations from the insurance company—and may thus be the one that owes the tax, even under present laws.

4. Another possibility being given consideration is the imposition of a companion tax to the insurance premium tax, which would cover the use of insurance in New York to protect against risks in the state. The basis of this tax would be similar

to that of the use tax which supplements the sales tax on retail sales. This concept would possibly avoid the constitutional problems that Texas and some other states have encountered, which culminated in the *Todd Shipyard* case.[2] This will not be proposed in the immediate future but is something that could develop within the next few years.

5. New York officials are also considering an eventual increase in the amount of supervision given noninsured employee welfare plans. Employees working for a firm which avoids taxes deserve the same protection and assurance as any other employees, that their benefits are soundly financed.

6. We are also considering several possible changes in taxes on insurance companies as a means of recovering any revenue losses that may eventually occur through tax avoidance.

7. Finally, we are trying to get the insurance companies in New York to join with the state in seeking federal legislation outlawing discriminatory taxation of insurance companies. This practice is obviously detrimental, both to New York and to the insurance companies which are an important part of our economy.

In closing, I must admit that after more than six years of study, we have not yet developed satisfactory solutions to the insurance tax problems centering around employee welfare benefits. We are continuing to study these problems and our State Administration solicits your suggestions.

---

[2] State Board of Insurance et al, v. Todd Shipyards Corporation, 370 U.S. 451, 8 L. ed. 2nd 620, 82 S. Ct. 1380 (1962).

CHAPTER VII

DISCUSSION OF TAXES AND BENEFIT PLANS FOR EMPLOYEES GENERALLY[1]

Chairman Robert E. Royes, American Telephone and Telegraph Company: We now come to the discussion part of our program. These discussions are records, and they constitute an important part of the published symposium volume. Therefore, in asking a question or making a comment, please identify yourself.

Mr. John E. Patton, Carpenter, Bennett & Morrissey, Newark: Mr. Henderson, my question is this. If you are drafting a savings plan along the lines of a pension plan, where the company is making a contribution regardless of accumulated earnings or current earnings, can you also provide in your plan that after a certain period of years, even if the employee still continues in employment with the company, he can withdraw part of those company contributions, even though it is not geared as a profit-sharing plan?

Mr. C. R. Henderson, Johnson & Higgins, New York: The question is: In a 401 (a) plan, which is technically a pension plan, can an employee at any time in his career while still employed, withdraw money which was attributable to employer contributions? It is my understanding that he cannot do that. The answer is to make the plan a profit-sharing plan as suggested in my talk.

If you want to have something in the shape of a savings-type plan to which you put money for the employee's account, and you do make it technically a pension plan rather than a profit-sharing plan, you can grade the employer's contribution, with age, as you cannot do in a profit-sharing plan. You can say 2 per cent of pay

---

[1] EDITORIAL NOTE: The arrangement of chapters in this volume differs slightly from the order of presentation at the symposium. This chapter includes discussion of the paper on "Growth of Pension Funds and Economic Implications" which was given at the same session, but does not include discussion of the paper by Mr. Kenneth C. Foster, which was given at a dinner meeting.

for a guy up to, say, 40 years old and then 4 per cent of pay between 40 and 50, 6 per cent between 50 and 60, 7 and 8 per cent between 60 and 65. This grading with age means that you will be able to provide approximately the same rate of retirement income for a 25-year-old out of this year's contributions as you do for a 64-year-old.

Mrs. Janet L. Hoffman, Baltimore City Council Fiscal Adviser: In Baltimore we are soon to undertake a series of negotiations between labor organizations and the representative groups working for the city government. Pension policy will be one of the items to be negotiated.

My question concerns the relative role of social security on the one hand, as compared with pensions on the other hand, in meeting cost-of-living changes as they may occur, both before and after retirement. I understand from the discussion, that there may be a difference between the two with respect to their role in adjusting to cost-of-living changes and in the tax treatment of such changes. Our pension system policies for over 35,000 employees may have considerable bearing upon what we can successfully get put through the negotiation process.

I would like Mr. David to comment on what role federal social security should be expected to serve in the way of making changes in the cost of living over the years as opposed to the role of the private pension plan.

Mr. Alvin M. David, United States Social Security Administration: Well, that is an interesting question right now. By reason of the statements by Mr. Nixon and Mr. Humphrey that I just mentioned, and also by reason of what is said in the Democratic and the Republican platforms, it appears that unless the Congress is against the proposal there will be a provision in the social security law for automatic adjustment of social security benefits to the cost of living.

We now have automatic adjustments of civil service retirement pay, and there is provision for automatic adjustment of military retirement pay. There is none in social security, but over the years, on an ad hoc basis, social security benefits have been adjusted from time to time, with the result that they have actually more than kept up with the cost of living.

84

The big thing that can be said about an automatic provision is that it would deal with the problem routinely without Congressional action. In other words, it would be handled administratively. When the cost of living went up by, say, 1 per cent, we would increase the benefits accordingly. We cannot do it more often than once a year. But, with computers, even with our 24 million beneficiaries, we could revise the benefits automatically once a year when the cost of living so indicated.

Even though on a long-term basis, with jumps from time to time, social security adjustments have kept up, there have been lags, and sometimes these lags are quite long; for example, there was an interval between 1958 and 1965 where there was no increase—where the beneficiaries went without any adjustment to the cost of living. And no adjustment made afterwards, of course, will take care of filling that gap. Those were years when the retired person had less to eat and less to make do with.

The automatic increase in social security that has been proposed by both parties and both candidates can be provided for without changing the contribution rates. Wages go up by considerably more than the cost of living, and the income to the social security system therefore also increases, and it will increase by considerably more than enough to meet the cost-of-living changes without the necessity for a change in the contribution rate.

President F. Cleveland Hedrick, Jr., Hedrick and Lane, Washington, D.C.: On this last point, would not this require some elasticity in the ceiling, and is that a part of it?

Mr. David: Yes. One thing that I should have added is that if the ceiling of $7,800 is not revised, after a while increases in wages will not make any difference to the income of the system because everybody will be getting $7,800 or more, and further increases in wages will not increase the income to the system. So it is necessary that the ceiling be increased from time to time if automatic adjustments are going to be financed without changing the contribution rate.

Mr. John C. Pyle, Jr., Metropolitan Life Insurance Company: Obviously in a few minutes, I could not even begin to comment briefly on what Lloyd has said here. I must say that he and I are good friends and that we have had areas of agreement from time to time, as we have areas of disagreement. I have no doubt that this pattern will continue in the future.

Under the present circumstances, however, I feel under some constraint to say that the opinion of Attorney General Louis J. Lefkowitz, which was issued on December 27, 1966, with respect to what Lloyd refers to as Met-Cat and which also referred to similar plans of other insurance companies, was correct; and if the new minimum premium plan, which he referred to as Mini-Met, is submitted to the attorney general for opinion also, I am sure that the attorney general will reach the correct conclusion just as he did on Met-Cat, because basically I think there is really no legal difference between the two. There are some differences of practice.

Another thing I might say is that a 2 per cent premium tax might sound like a very small matter. However, when that is compared with a tax on an allocated portion of the life insurance company's federal taxable income, it amounts to a net income tax of about 22 to 34 per cent—that is, in the state of New York—and that does not compare very favorably with the current net income tax on other corporations of 7 per cent.

One of the things that happens under the retaliatory statutes of other states, which the domestic New York companies are so concerned about now, results from the premium tax increase enacted in New York this year. At the beginning of this year the rates were increased for New York companies by a quarter of a per cent. On life insurance premiums the rate went up from 1.75 per cent to 2 per cent and on accident and health insurance it went up from 2 per cent to 2.25 per cent.

Now, this has not occurred yet with respect to companies doing business in New York but domiciled in other states. Their rates would go up to those same figures as of July 1, 1969. This would raise the rates sufficiently high that the New York companies doing business in other states—and there are now 45 other states, 46 including New York, which have these horrendous retaliatory statutes that Lloyd spoke of—would be required by reason of this increase due July 1, 1969, to pay automatically additional taxes to 45 other states.

To give you an example: Metropolitan paid premium tax to New York State on its 1967 business of over $8 million. This new rate increase would increase that tax to over $9 million a year, assuming that the premium income does not change from year to year, but it obviously will. In addition, without any other legislature lifting a finger, my company would have to pay above $4 million to 45 other states. This is a nice way to get revenue so far as the other states are concerned, but we prefer that they do not get it out of us.

I must say that I agree completely, Lloyd, with your statements about the "Blues" and the noninsured versus insured benefit plans. I think that there is too much tax discrimination in favor of noninsured plans. I am also interested to learn all of these other things that you are thinking about, and I am sure that we shall find many areas of agreement and areas of disagreement, and in the latter I hope that I can have some influence on your thinking.

Mr. James N. Ravlin, Brown & Williamson Tobacco Corporation: I wonder if one of the speakers might elect to comment on the concept of variable annuities and also its counterpart for social security taking in the cost-of-living increases. I am asking about setting a rate, its counterpart for social security, taking in the cost-of-living increases.

Mr. Henderson: It is a sort of philosophical question. I shall just speak for myself for a minute.

Over the time it takes to earn and spend a pension, prices have always changed and changed a lot. There are two ways of really going at that. Of course you can theoretically update past service or increase pensions for pensioners. But if you are going to do something about it automatically, without constant legislative adjustments, one thing you can do is to tie things to a cost-of-living index. The other thing is to give the participants an investment position in a fund invested in equities.

Well, I think, the first one has all kinds of difficulties. In the first place, it starts putting the emphasis in an expensive program on need. I don't want to knock need. It is important. We all want to look at it. But when you start saying, "We are going to give people what they need" without looking at the means for providing it, somewhere down the road something has got to give.

If, on the other hand, you give people an investment position in the type of equity portfolio that you would hope they would work out if they had their own investment position, that will work out pretty well.

Variable annuities are not really so very new. Long Island Lighting has had a plan like this in effect since 1952. Many business corporations have had trusteed variable annuities for the last decade and a half. The College Retirement Equities Fund has been in business since 1952. The insurance companies are now rapidly moving into not just the variable annuity field but also the equity field, because the word has gotten around—through one thing or another, partly a financial columnist, partly a mutual fund salesman going out—that if you have a long-range financial program it is short-sighted to put it all in bonds. That is all we are talking about. I think this movement is now going to bloom very rapidly because it has been incubating for a long time.

History shows that with almost any idea, it comes along, somebody tries it, it is talked about a lot, and then after quite a while it becomes widespread. The proof of this right now is that if you go back two years you could number on the thumb of one hand the large insurance companies that were interested in any equity product. Now we have several dozen who have applications, registration statements pending before the Securities and Exchange Commission in Washington to sell individual variable annuities and to sell mutual funds. Of course, in addition to this development we have quite a number of large insurance companies now ready and active in selling group variable annuities for employees.

Miss Marcia K. Marshall, Port of New York Authority: I would like to ask Mr. Henderson whether there is not something new in the Internal Revenue Service about getting term life insurance out from minimum sharing or minimum assigned rights.

Mr. Henderson: Yes, there is a recent revenue ruling.

For quite a long while it has been possible for an individual to take an individual life insurance policy, assign it to his wife and, if he did it long enough before he died, this took it out of his estate for federal estate tax purposes, even though he continued to pay the premium. This goes back some years. If you go back a little further, you find Internal Revenue Code provisions which make that question depend on who paid the premium.

This procedure was not generally considered available for group life insurance, however. In reaching the conclusion that employees were not taxable on the current protection of group term life protection, Internal Revenue Service said it was a small amount, the employee did not have any ownership in it, and he did not have anything to assign. Lots of group life policies said, "You can't assign the insurance." However, for quite a long while many insurance companies have permitted, or did not argue, when an employee assigned his group life insurance; and a number of estates have actually been administered on the proposition that when an executive or other employee died who had assigned the group life to his wife before he died, that insurance was not considered part of his estate.

Very recently—this year—the Internal Revenue Service issued a ruling which said, "If you assign your group life insurance, it is out of your estate. However, you have to make sure that under the applicable state laws you can really assign it, and you have to assign everything, and this includes the right to convert."

Well, the industry breathed a little easier when this thing came out. There are fewer questions about whether you can assign group life insurance, but a tough reviewer in the Internal Revenue Service can still say, "In your state could the insurance be assigned? In your state could the right to convert be assigned?" All I can say is, it is better than it was.

Now, if you really want to be sure that you would get this insurance out of the estate, use one of these individual policies which I just described.

Mr. Herman C. Biegel, Lee, Toomey & Kent, Washington, D.C.: Mr. Chairman, I would like to ask a question of Professor Holland.

I am not sure whether it appears in a later portion of your paper, Professor, but in Table 1 you indicate the total number of employees in all industries except government and agriculture who are covered—which I take to mean 50,700,000—and then your next line says "Percentage covered" in terms of a percentage. That is 50.1 per cent. Do you have any idea of how many of those covered, namely, half of the working force, will ever receive pensions?

I don't mean to pre-empt tomorrow morning's session on concepts of vesting, et cetera, but one of the basic points made by

Secretary W. Willard Wirtz and other members of the Administration is that while a large number of employees are technically covered by private pension plans, very few of them—and what constitutes "very few" is questionable—ever receive benefits under those plans.

Professor Daniel M. Holland, Massachusetts Institute of Technology: In the past, if I had been asked something like this, I would have drawn on all the expertise at my command, which was an estimate made by Dan McGill some time back to the effect that, to the best of his educated guessing, about half of those currently covered by plans will never meet the vesting and/or age requirements of the plan they are currently covered by, but even that educated guess is a foxy answer in the sense that they will go to other plans and may in fact get benefits under those, which is an academic way of saying that I have no answer to your question.

President Hedrick: I am sorry to come up so many times but I wonder if I could ask Dr. Slater a question. What has been the reception of the Mini-Met or whatever you call it, by various names, in other states? Do you know how it has been going there?

Dr. Lloyd E. Slater, New York State Deputy Commissioner for Tax Research: I shall comment on the question, and I would be pleased, John, if you want to supplement what I shall say.

The only thing that I know definitely is that the state of Missouri took action against the Monsanto Chemical Company,[2] which went into one of these plans, and the case has been languishing somewhere in the courts for five years, at least. At the same time they took an action against the Schlitz Brewing Company,[3] which has an establishment in Kansas City, that was so-called self-insured. They apparently felt in the Schlitz case that the company was actually conducting an insurance business and, therefore, should be meeting all the regulations for an insurance company, and this would include paying a premium tax. They also indicated that, in their opinion, Monsanto had been able to enter into a contract that relieved its insurer of some of the tax and had in so doing

---

[2] Pending in St. Louis County Circuit Court—State of Missouri ex rel. Ralph H. Duggins v. Monsanto Company (1964).

[3] Pending in St. Louis County Circuit Court—State of Missouri ex. rel. Ralph H. Duggins v. Jos. Schlitz Brewing Co. (1964).

also become an insurance company subject to regulations and taxes.

For some reason those cases have been very slow in moving and at last report had not moved at all.

I know of no state, though, that has taken action that to any extent takes care of these problems.

There are 25 states that are discriminating and are, therefore, creating pressure on Metropolitan and the rest of the companies in this state to try to do something so they can compete in those other states. That is what is really involved here, in my opinion. Those states are not going to be too sympathetic to changing any of their positions and I don't see any hope for a solution to these problems until there is some federal action, and I don't see any hope for that either until we can get some cooperation between some of the industry in those states that are being hurt by this and the states themselves. John, do you want to comment?

Mr. Pyle: Just a word. Those two cases that Lloyd mentioned did not involve taxes at all. They involved merely the question of whether or not the employer was in the insurance business. Those cases have proceeded very, very slowly in the courts and my last information is that they will be continued indefinitely, which I assume means that the state is giving up.

I think that this is such a political thing that the insurance department, in my own opinion, might have preferred not to have started the cases in the first place, because there have been no other cases, no other instances, of any enforcement of additional premium taxes on Metropolitan or any other company that I know of in any state as to these minimum premium plans. That is my latest information on it. But several state insurance departments have made announcements at various times on the subject, and at the present time Metropolitan is involved in litigating the question in several states as to whether or not the state insurance department must approve the Mini-Met form. We have one of those cases going in Connecticut and another in Illinois.

Dr. Slater: May I just add: I do think that even though the Missouri case did not actually involve taxes, an assessment for the tax obligation would have become quite obvious if those particular cases had ever been decided favorably to the state. Otherwise, I think John has probably described the situation accurately. The delay there indicates some political problems, I suspect, more than judicial.

He has also spoken on the other point that I got up to comment on. In New York we have approved the form of the policy. We take the position here at least that Metropolitan could not have written this form without our approval. We did approve the form with the stipulation that our approval did not in any way imply that there would be any change in the tax status. We have not yet made any decision on what we shall eventually do. We are still trying to find out what the attorney general will decide our position should be with the insurance company, and we shall subsequently decide what position to take with the employers involved. The whole question is still open.

I take it from what you said, John, that very few other states have actually approved your form.

Mr. Pyle: Many states actually have approved the form.

Dr. Slater: Okay. I wasn't sure.

Mr. Pyle: The Met-Cat type forms were submitted for approval in only four states and were approved, but my recollection is that the Mini-Met form has been approved in practically all of the states where approval is required.

Chairman Royes: Mr. David has a comment on a comment. We are turning into a panel, perhaps. This has to do with the question of how many people actually get benefits, and I believe he has a comment he would like to make on Professor Holland's comment.

Mr. David: Professor Holland made one brief reference to social security financing that I appreciate having the opportunity to make a comment on myself. That was the professor's remark on the fact—and it is a fact—that if social security were not adequately financed, the government, with its taxing power, could increase the taxes. Then he said, of course, beyond that they could even go ahead and print money. Well, of course, that is true, too, but you really ought to say that up to now the financing of social security has been handled in the most scrupulous way by the committees in Congress responsible for it, and they have used very conservative financing assumptions. In other words, the financing of the social security cash benefits is based on the assumption that wages will not go up one dime from the year 1966, which is the base of the current estimate, and that the ceiling, now $7,800, on the amount of earnings subject to tax under social security, will not go up a dime. Thus, the program is financed quite conservatively in this respect, and in all other respects the committees have done it in a way to be as sure as they can, as sure as it is possible for anybody to be, that the financing that is in the present law will be sufficient to cover the cost of the system for the next 75 years, and that is on the assumption that there are no increases in wages.

Chairman Royes: I would like to ask Professor Holland a question, too, from an economic viewpoint:

The thing that bothers me about these automatic adjustments of large-scale things to the cost of living is what it does economically to the rest of the country who don't have any opportunity to benefit from automatic adjustment to the cost of living.

Do you want to address yourself to that for a second?

Professor Holland: The question is: What kind of problems are posed in the way of disparities when adjustments are made to the cost of living in connection with some sectors of the community that are not open to other sectors of the community? The answer, I suppose, is not really strictly an economic one. The answer is that more discontent than previously characterized our community will now exist in it and that some kinds of occupations and functions will become less desired and others more desired.

It is the same question that affects what kind of businesses to get into, those that involve long-run commitments with assumptions therein about stability of prices and those that involve quick turnovers with almost automatic protections against price increases. I think the question is an even deeper one, and that is whether some of the so-called cost-of-living adjustments that are now being relied on will in fact have that characteristic.

I have no concern that the government will not exercise its powers in the most conservative financial ways, yet, parenthetically, I distinguish between government and business as a pedagogical point, and also because some governments, other governments, foreign governments, have not always followed the careful social security financing of our government.

While the government has the power to stay abreast of such movements, it has been implicitly assumed that equities, or common stocks, will give us an equivalent power in the private sector, and that is based on past experience and an empirical regularity, but it is not based on any certainty of any sort that such a relationship will in fact continue.

Many businesses are committing themselves to the equivalent of cost-of-living adjustments in final-year formulas for pension plans but nobody can really say anything about their ability to finance them in any real way.

So that ultimately, I think—this sounds terribly corny—faith is at the base of some of the adjustments.

Chairman Royes: Thank you very much. I think we are going to have to close now in order that we may get in to luncheon on time.

Mr. Biegel: May I end this morning's session with a word of sincere thanks to all the panelists and Mr. Royes. It shows how great those of us who select these speakers can be made to look. While we had hoped for an excellent program, these gentlemen have even excelled our brightest expectations.

Thank you all for contributing very substantially to this morning's program.

PART THREE

HOW TAXES AFFECT BENEFIT PLANS
FOR EXECUTIVES

"Probably many of you have been to a number of sessions which have involved executive compensation. I think we have something a little different this afternoon in that first we are going to hear a summary of how we tax experts have been going about trying to achieve some kind of tax amelioration for our executives; and then we are going to hear, for the first time, at least to my knowledge, an exposé of how successful we have been in the past.

"We have planned to keep the major presentations and panel discussions relatively short, in order to have a maximum amount of time for participation from the floor."

—Roy A. Wentz, Jr.
Chief Counsel, Federal and Foreign
Tax Division, E. I. du Pont de
Nemours & Company

CHAPTER VIII

DEVELOPMENT OF
EXECUTIVE COMPENSATION PATTERNS

V. Henry Rothschild, 2nd
Attorney, New York

I AM GOING to direct myself primarily to an important phenomenon of this business era—mergers, consolidations, and take-overs—and their effects on compensation programs. I think the possibility of merger has to be kept in mind today in the preparation of a compensation program, not only for the many companies that are susceptible to merger—to use a more delicate term than the usual "take-over" phrase—but also for the acquiring company.

The Effect of a Merger

Last week I had lunch with a retired executive who was formerly a major executive of a large corporation. Over a period of years I had worked on a number of plans for his company: incentive compensation or bonus plans, a stock option and stock purchase plan, a series of amendments to the company's pension plan, a profit-sharing plan (put in largely at the instance of the union but which nevertheless had definite benefits for executives), and deferred compensation plans in various forms—in general, the patterns of executive compensation incentives that are prevalent today.

The company had prospered. The incentive compensation plan had produced substantial amounts and, as the executive had approached retirement age, a large portion of the awards that had been made to him had been deferred and had been made payable in company stock—first, over a 10-year period and then, as the amounts grew larger, over 15 years. The stock payments had been translated into so-called restricted stock, which has become the seventh wonder of the world.

The stock option plan had been unusually successful for this executive. From a price of $32 a share, at which the option had been granted, the stock had risen to $90, then split two for one. The split stock continued to rise, so that for a stock with a cost basis of $16 after the stock split, the owner had shares at the time he retired with a value of $72, or more than four times what he had paid.

Apart from the stock plan, he had managed to save some money and buy additional company stock of his own at a relatively low price. He still owned much stock, after gifts to members of his family, although he had a pretty heavy loan outstanding which had been incurred to enable him to purchase the stock. It was initially a character loan that later was secured with some of the stock.

To make matters more interesting, in a merger that had taken place after he had retired, the stock of his company had been exchanged for securities of another corporation, and the securities he held, as a result, had a value of $85, a further increase of $13.

You might conclude that this executive was sitting pretty! Here was a man who had devoted his entire working life to one company, had become one of its principal executives, and had helped that company to success. You would think through the plans just mentioned, coupled with some intelligent estate planning, he would be receiving his just reward—an estate that would produce enough income to enable him to live comfortably during his years of retirement, with adequate provision for his widow and children thereafter. But what were the facts?

The facts were that he had to borrow a substantial sum to meet the next payments of his federal, New York State, and New York City estimated income taxes (which by that time had been increased by the federal surtax.) Moreover, there were serious and justifiable questions in his mind as to whether there would be enough after his death to provide properly for his widow, his children, and an unmarried niece who was wholly dependent on him.

Now, how could that be, one would ask. The tax-oriented will not say, as most others would, "Well, he must have spent his money foolishly. He gambled on the market or at Las Vegas. He married too often. He lived extravagantly." None of these things was true. He had hardly invested at all except in his company's stock and a modest amount in tax-exempts; he had no alimony to pay; he did not live extravagantly in terms of what was expected of an individual in his circumstances—certainly no more extravagantly than people with his income live today, although, like most of us, he had been spending sums he was receiving without making adequate provision for the April 15 day of reckoning.

Well, then, what had happened? A combination of events over which he had no real control, principally the fact that when the merger took place, apparently increasing the value of his stock by 13 points, the merger took what has currently become a popular form, a non-tax-free exchange of debentures plus stock for his company's stock—believed to be an installment sale, to be sure, but none the less taxable. This is what happened:

First, of course, the profit on all the stock the executive owned became taxable to him. Had he held it, as he had planned to do, there would have been no tax during his lifetime and, under present tax rules, no income tax on a large profit after his death. With his low-cost base, an enforced sale as an incident of merger depleted his assets by well over 15 per cent of the major part of his estate represented by the stock which he had earned and bought during his employment.

Second, with company stock he had set up a trust for his wholly dependent niece. The income had been made payable to her during her lifetime, but since his estate needed assets and a substantial gift tax would have been entailed, terms of the trust provided that on her death the remainder was to return to his estate; the trust, in effect, terminated on her death. Again, it was contemplated that at least during his lifetime the stock, which was producing a good income, would not be sold. The taxable exchange incident to the merger, however, resulted in his liability for capital gains taxes on paper profits of the trust, with no securities in his hands that he could sell, to pay the taxes.

Third, he had also set up irrevocable trusts for his children with company stock. His children were not affluent, and they had long counted on the income from the trust. Even though the new securities paid a higher return, the capital gains tax which the trust had to pay so reduced the principal of the trust that the income was less than it had been before.

An additional factor contributing to the situation was that deferred compensation was being used up as the executive continued to live, and because of the income taxes on his pension and on the dividends from his stock, he was unable to save.

Also, on the death of his niece or on his death, the stock was to come back to his estate. To provide for his niece he had elected a joint and survivor annuity under his pension plan, with a $10,000 annuity payable to her. That had been a fine and adequate amount many years ago, but with the inflation of 4 per cent a year or more which is currently taking place, he felt, and with some justification, that she could no longer live on that amount.

Problem of Non-Tax-Free Exchanges

Now, what is the moral of this particular situation?

For one thing, non-tax-free exchanges may look good in terms of increases in value and increases in income, but for employees with low-cost bases for their stock, as with stockholders with low-cost bases generally, they can produce real hardship.

Second, the hardships for employed executives and other employees can be even more serious. For example, consider the actual case of certain executives, with qualified stock options which had been exercised a year or two before, who found as a result of exchange of stock at time of merger that their holding period of three years was destroyed. They became subject to ordinary income tax on the spread between the market value of the stock and the option price at the time they had purchased it.

In the case of unexercised qualified options, bonds or debentures cannot be substituted, because only stock can be made subject to qualified stock options. Stock of the new company, therefore, had to be substituted. This presented two serious problems:

First, the executives were, in effect, being offered something different from what stockholders generally were being offered and, irrespective of values, this can always be subject to criticism.

Second, of course, there is the question of the valuation of stock when a company acquires another, or merges with another, and a new stock option is issued. If you offer the same stock to all stockholders, then of course you have a basis for valuation. If you pick a select group, you have a heavy burden to show market value immediately after and immediately before, within the tax rules.

OTHER PROBLEMS RAISED BY MERGERS

Other questions that can be raised by mergers and acquisitions are: What assurance can there be that there will be no reduction in pension benefits? How can you continue incentive compensation and plans based on sharing profits?

Termination of employment, if it is not properly handled, can trigger the payment of deferred compensation or the lapse of options, or the loss of pension rights.

The problems presented by acquisitions and mergers are to me the most important current problems of executive compensation today, for two reasons: Relatively few companies now are free from the threat of possible acquisition. (A large company or a company with a concentration of blocks of stock may be, but many, many companies, even very large companies, are not.) Second, even a large company must be concerned, because of the uncertainty created in the minds of executives and the disturbance created in terms of what is going to happen, as a result of a merger, to benefits that have been created for them over a period of years.

EMPLOYMENT AGREEMENTS

This is a challenge that can be met and is being increasingly met by employment agreements, which have become an increasingly important aspect of the phenomenon of mergers and consolidations.

Employment agreements, of course, have long been used as a form for an agreement by the employee to turn over to the company inventions and discoveries. They have also long been used as consideration for stock options, but this is a matter of consideration supplied by the employee.

101

They have been used in connection with deferred compensation under agreements such as one providing that following termination of employment an employee will receive a sum equal to $5,000 for every year worked.

Employment agreements are sometimes used for individual profit-sharing agreements, but this is on an annual basis. One company has numerous such agreements, but the right to terminate is on three months' notice.

Most of these agreements are, in effect, unilateral. The company retains the right to terminate. The binding employment contract has been rare, except in the case of an executive who has been hired from another company and who wants some guarantee of the benefits that he will receive.

Today, however, an increasing number of companies are adopting employment agreements for most of their top executives. Many ask, "How good are they?" In the first place, the individual whose employment has been terminated has to prove damages. He has to show, under the common law, that he tried to look for something comparable and could not find it and that his present job is paying him less. Then there is the expense of litigation, if there is a hostile management.

Also, there are more ways than one of firing a man. I am a member of the national panel of the American Arbitration Association, and one case which I was called on to arbitrate involved a discharge—not discharge, actually. The individual concerned had an employment agreement, but what did the company do? It put the executive in a small office first, then gave his secretary some additional work for another man, and finally took her away altogether. Part of the correspondence that he was receiving was cut off and was assigned elsewhere. In other words, company management was trying to induce him to quit. There are, of course, more ways than one of firing.

New Forms of Agreement

New forms of agreement, however, are now being developed to meet these points, and ingenuity is being displayed. Special problems arise when a person is an officer, because we cannot provide that a person who is an officer will continue to be one after a change in control of the company. We can provide that if an individual is not elected an officer he will receive, by way of severance pay or otherwise, some fixed amount, and this is basically the type of provision that is being used: namely, a provision for severance pay or liquidated damages, with a provision for continuance of salary for a designated period, pension payments equivalent to what he would have received, payable not all at one time but in installments, and an important provision that if there is a change in management and he reasonably believes that he cannot work compatibly with the new management, he will be entitled to severance pay.

The validity of these agreements has not been tested, but an agreement of this nature at least puts the executive in a negotiating position. For such agreements, I have recommended an arbitration clause. There are, of course, disadvantages to arbitration. A basic disadvantage is that arbitrators usually take a bottom figure and a top figure and split the difference—that is the frequent and practical method of dispensing justice in arbitration proceedings. In favor of arbitration, you find that it is speedy, that it involves far less expense, and that you may fairly expect some payment if you have got a fair and reasonable agreement.

A New Pattern of Executive Compensation

Every period creates its own challenges. The principal challenge today is in creating new patterns of compensation which will provide for the take-over, friendly or unfriendly. It is a field calling for imagination and new forms of protection for successful management. This is how patterns of executive compensation develop, and it is in this area, in particular, that a new pattern of executive compensation is beginning to develop today.

CHAPTER IX

TAX MINIMIZATION AND EXECUTIVE COMPENSATION PLANS

Wilbur G. Lewellen
*Associate Professor of Industrial Management,
Herman C. Krannert Graduate School of
Industrial Administration, Purdue University*

IN VIRTUALLY every discussion of the impact of taxes on employee benefit plans, one category of employee—the senior corporate executive—is singled out for particular attention. The levels of compensation commonly associated with positions of this sort clearly are of a magnitude that encourages policies to be guided by tax planning considerations of one kind or another. Despite the widespread recognition of this phenomenon, however, our economic analysis of its dimensions and consequences has lagged behind the accounting and legal expertise which has been applied to the technical details of the process of remuneration.

We have all been vaguely aware that taxes have induced significant changes in the structure of executive rewards during the last quarter century, but the precise extent of those changes, their impact on executives' effective tax rates, and the degree to which corporations have taken advantage of the room to maneuver which differential tax burdens permit, have not thus far been subjected to hard analysis. My objective here this afternoon is to remedy at least part of that deficiency, both by reporting the results of some recent empirical studies of the executive pay package which I have undertaken for the National Bureau of Economic Research, and by outlining certain extensions of those studies that bear directly on the activity we may loosely term "tax minimization."

THE EMPIRICAL EVIDENCE

One of the major problems in assessing the character of the executive compensation transaction lies in the fact that only a portion of the rewards at issue—direct cash salary and bonus payments—are readily observable and conveniently measured. Payments of this sort are, of course, prominently reported on in corporate proxy statements. Those devices which tax considerations have been most influential in encouraging, however—pensions, deferred compensation, profit-sharing, stock purchase plans, and stock options—are similarly reported but give rise to levels of remuneration that are clear only upon quite extensive supplementary analysis. Unless and until that analysis is made, speculation about developments in executive pay cannot be very meaningful.

With this in mind, the National Bureau of Economic Research incorporated a study to provide the requisite information in its project on Tax Policies for Economic Growth. The study, of which I was the author, concentrated on the compensation experience of the top five executives in what are essentially the 50 largest industrial corporations in the United States. It covered the period from 1940 to 1963, thereby encompassing the interval wherein the transition from low to high marginal personal tax rates took place in this country. A total of some 550 different executives and approximately 8,000 man-years of compensation data were ultimately included in the investigation. Proxy statements provided the raw material.

The task of the study was to develop and apply a series of techniques that would permit the remuneration implied by the various deferred and contingent items in the executive compensation package to be measured and compared with the observed direct cash payments. The conceptual approach chosen consisted of determining an index denoted the "current income equivalent" of each supplement to salary and bonus. In the case of pension plans, for example, the question was posed: "How large an increase in annual salary would the prospective pension recipient require in order to be able to purchase therewith an individual retirement annuity contract from an insurance company, similar in form and equal in value to the benefits promised him under his company's retirement plan?"

That annual salary increase specifies, in effect, the amount of additional current income the executive could accept in lieu of his pension commitment and still guarantee himself the same level of economic security in retirement. As such, it can be compared to his actual salary for purposes of evaluating the relative importance of the pension. Once the other deferred and contingent arrangements he enjoys are similarly translated into current income values, their total defines the worth of the aggregate pay package, and its composition can then be analyzed with some confidence.

The details of the procedures developed for this purpose are sufficiently complex that I will simply refer those of you who are interested to the study itself for their description.[1] Clearly, it was necessary to deal not only with numerous provisions of the tax laws relating to employee benefits, but also to incorporate adjustments for vesting, death benefit payments, mortality, time deferral, and the vagaries of stock price movements over time in the instance of devices whose payoffs took the form of shares of the employer firm's common stock.

Throughout, however, two principles in particular were carefully adhered to in making the necessary calculations: first, that "equivalence" between a possible series of salary payments, on the one hand, and a given compensation scheme, on the other, be always defined in terms of the after-tax *present values* of the two; second, that every "current income equivalent" thus created be designed in such a way that it could be utilized, in fact, as an alternative in an actual package of executive rewards. In short, the concept of the "time value of money" and a persistent attempt to be practical played significant roles in the analysis. Both permit some conclusions to be drawn about effective tax rates and the minimizing of effective tax burdens.

---

[1] W. G. Lewellen, *Executive Compensation in Large Industrial Corporations*, New York, Columbia University Press and National Bureau of Economic Research, 1968, 371 p. See especially, Chapters 2 through 6.

RESULTS OF THE STUDY

The outcome of the investigation is reported in full in the National Bureau book indicated,[2] and I shall therefore merely summarize a few of the more pertinent findings for our purposes here. It turned out that, while senior executive salaries and bonuses rose by some 80 per cent before taxes and 35 per cent after taxes, from 1940 to 1963, the value of the total compensation package slightly better than doubled. Surprisingly, these increases occurred almost entirely in the decade 1945 to 1955. Since 1955, both cash payments alone and total pay have stagnated.

As one might expect, the non-cash elements of the pay package grew quite rapidly in importance, especially in the 1950's. The magnitude of that growth, however, exceeded the typical expectation. During the period 1955 through 1963, salary and bonus accounted on average for only one-third of the aggregate remuneration enjoyed by the highest-paid executive in each of the 50 companies studied. For the top five executives combined, the corresponding figure was about 50 per cent. Clearly, salary and bonus payments no longer dominate the executive reward structure and, indeed, are in most instances actually minority components of the relevant income flows. By way of contrast, salary and bonus provided some 80 per cent of total earnings in the early 1940's. A key feature of many of the newer deferred and contingent compensation arrangements, of course, is their link to the market performance of the corporation's stock. In consequence, executives' rewards have become increasingly tied over time to the economic benefits enjoyed directly by their firms' shareholders. Between 1955 and 1963, such items as stock options, stock bonuses, stock purchase plans, profit-sharing plans, and stock deferred-pay arrangements generated one-third to one-half of total pay.

Similar results, it might be noted in passing, emerge from an examination of senior executive earnings in another sector of the economy—retailing. Dan Holland and I have just recently finished

---

[2] See also, for an abbreviated version: W. G. Lewellen, "Executives Lose Out, Even With Options," *Harvard Business Review*, 46 (January-February, 1968), 127-142.

the calculations for a sample consisting of the 15 largest retailers in the country, and find a shift of approximately the same dimensions since 1940 toward deferred and contingent forms of compensation. Apparently, therefore, the kinds of comparisons I would like to offer for your comment have an applicability which is not limited to the particular firms on whose experience I shall focus at the moment.

EFFECTIVE TAX RATES

One of those comparisons has to do with the impact of supplements to salary and bonus on the effective overall tax rate paid by executives on their aggregate remuneration. What, after all, is the tax burden in practice on this package of rewards which is weighted so heavily in the direction of non-cash items? To that end, let me use as an illustration the average experience of the executives in the large manufacturing sample during the period 1955 through 1963. The "typical" man—i.e., a composite of the men who occupied all five top positions in the 50 firms studied—enjoyed average annual before-tax salary and bonus payments amounting to $135,000. After taxes, considering the likely extent of his taxable income from other sources—which affects his marginal bracket— and taking into account deductions and exemptions at a level IRS data indicate was common at his income level, the resulting after-tax annual salary and bonus average was $67,000. Thus, the effective tax rate on his cash income was almost exactly 50 per cent.

Since this $67,000 represented only 52 per cent of the total $129,000 value of his yearly pay, however, his overall experience was rather more favorable. Taxes on his prospective pension and deferred compensation benefits, while assessed at ordinary income rates, were postponed until such time as the payments were actually received and therefore were diminished in present value terms. In addition, his stock option earnings and any profit-sharing or other rewards payable in a lump sum at retirement received capital gains treatment besides being deferred. On the basis of the typical man's age, and assuming he would not sell the shares acquired under options until at least seven years subsequent to the date of the option grant,[3] the effective tax rate on the 48 per cent of his compensation which consisted of noncurrent rewards came to just 24 per cent. Combining this with the burden on cash income, the resulting overall effective rate turns out to have been 37.5 per cent. Despite the high level of total pay involved, then, the progressiveness of the personal income tax schedule was sidestepped by firms to a degree that allowed the executive to keep almost two-thirds of his before-tax earnings.

This finding compares favorably with the data Pechman has presented showing that effective tax rates for above-$50,000 income recipients, in general, run from 26 to 29 per cent under the 1964 Revenue Act—which, of course, specifies statutory rates lower than those in effect during the 1955-1963 period cited here for executives.[4] Even though most high-income individuals would have very heavy capital gains, whereas corporate executives' incomes would be expected to be weighted more heavily toward direct cash income, the latter group has not been subjected to significantly worse tax treatment after all.

A still better feeling for the tax-ameliorating capacities of supplements to salary and bonus can be obtained by looking at the compensation transaction from a somewhat different viewpoint. The question may be asked: "What would the overall effective tax rate on executives have been, had their employers been forced to provide the full amount of the observed $129,000 annual after-tax income between 1955 and 1963 by salary and bonus *alone?*" If our tax laws had not made various deferred and contingent pay arrangements available on favorable terms, an average annual before-tax salary of fully $734,000 for the typical senior corporate executive would have been required during the period at issue.[5] The effective tax rate on that transaction would therefore have been 82.5 per cent, leaving $129,000 as take-home pay. The 37.5 per cent actual figure clearly looks rather generous by this standard.

---

[3] A figure which represents the average holding period of the option recipients in the sample studied.

[4] Joseph A. Pechman, *Federal Tax Policy*, Washington, Brookings Institution, 1966, pp. 65-66, 284.

[5] Lewellen, *op. cit. supra* note 1, pp. 145-153.

EFFECTIVE RATES AT DIFFERENT LEVELS

It is also of interest to inquire whether effective rates of taxation change significantly as the levels of remuneration involved for the executive increase. Is it true, for example, that the highest-paid man in a firm pays a greater percentage of his pre-tax earnings in taxes than do his less-well-rewarded subordinates? We, of course, would expect this to be the case, given a progressive tax schedule —but in fact that expectation is not met.

The explanation lies in the phenomenon that, as an individual advances to higher-paid positions within his firm, a growing percentage of his remuneration comes from non-cash items of one kind or another. Over the last 25 years, the salaries and bonuses of the second- through fifth-ranking executives in large corporations have grown more rapidly than those of the top man. *Aggregate* remuneration, however, has increased at the same pace for all five.[6] Obviously, deferred and contingent rewards have taken up the slack.

I mentioned earlier that salary and bonus accounted for approximately one-third of top executives' earnings in recent years, but came to one-half the total for the top-five group as a whole. This pattern has produced a situation wherein the anticipated higher marginal rates on larger incomes are almost precisely offset by the greater weight in the total of low-taxed devices. When one makes calculations of effective tax rates on the compensation of the highest-paid individual in each of the 50 firms studied, the result is a figure of 37.8 per cent for the period 1955-1963. This is almost embarrassingly close to the 37.5 per cent just indicated for the top five combined, despite the fact that the average total after-tax pay of the top man came to $211,000 as compared with $129,000 for all five. That finding suggests a degree of both rationality and care in compensation planning which I do not often see attributed to firms. Apparently they practice precisely what we would preach: As the desired level of remuneration rises, more of it is provided by utilizing supplements to salary and bonus rather than cash payments.

To complete the analogy, we may inquire again as to the magni-

---

[6] *Ibid,* pp. 187-203.

tude of the straight-salary figure that would have been necessary to achieve by that means alone the $211,000 after-tax income actually provided by all the various devices employed. For 1955 through 1963, an annual payment of $1,576,000 per capita would have been called for.[7] The effective rate of tax, accordingly, would have been 86.5 per cent instead of 37.8 per cent. Again, tax "loopholes" created considerable leverage.

Taxes and Company Costs

The tax-lightening opportunities inherent in an informed restructuring of the executive compensation package can be approached from yet another perspective. Just as it is possible for a corporation to reduce the personal tax burden on its employees by judicious use of indirect rewards, so is it possible for the firm to realize considerable savings in the cost to itself of providing a given desired level of remuneration. While I suspect none of you will be startled by an assertion that pure salary payments are not the most efficient form of compensation from a cost standpoint, I suspect also that we would not find general agreement among you regarding which devices *are* most efficient at different income-and-tax levels, nor about the extent to which corporations have in practice availed themselves of the optimum cost combination of possible rewards. Permit me therefore to offer some comparisons for your reaction.

Table 1 presents an analysis of the costs to the employer company of providing an additional dollar's worth of after-tax remuneration to an individual in the form of pension benefits, deferred compensation, or stock option profits, as a function of his base salary. The table specifies the relationships which held under the tax schedule in effect during the last decade of the empirical investigation I performed for the National Bureau, and duplicates those results for the statutory rates set by the Revenue Act of 1964. On the—perhaps unwarranted—belief that the current 10 per cent tax surcharge is only temporary, I have not included a comparison which incorporates the new rates.

The table should be read as follows, using the top line as an

---

[7] *Ibid.*, pp. 145-153.

TABLE 1

COST OF VARIOUS FRINGE BENEFITS AS A PERCENTAGE OF THE
COST OF AN EQUALLY-VALUABLE SALARY INCREASE

SALARY LEVEL	PENSIONS	DEFERRED COMPENSATION	STOCK OPTIONS
A. UNDER THE 1954-63 TAX SCHEDULE			
$ 15,000	67%	59%	172%
20,000	60	54	160
25,000	55	50	151
35,000	48	44	139
50,000	40	38	114
75,000	35	34	97
100,000	26	27	70
150,000	21	24	53
200,000	13	17	31
300,000	13	18	28
400,000	13	20	25
500,000	14	24	25
750,000	17	32	25
1,500,000	26	61	25

SALARY LEVEL	PENSIONS	DEFERRED COMPENSATION	STOCK OPTIONS
B. UNDER THE REVENUE ACT OF 1964			
$ 15,000	71%	61%	165%
20,000	65	57	156
25,000	61	54	150
35,000	55	49	141
50,000	48	44	128
75,000	44	40	115
100,000	38	38	97
150,000	35	38	87
200,000	33	39	77
300,000	35	43	77
400,000	36	49	77
500,000	38	54	77
750,000	40	60	77
1,500,000	43	68	77

illustration: The figure 67 per cent under "pensions" records the fact that a corporation would find it just 67 per cent as costly to use pension benefits to raise by one dollar the effective after-tax income of a man initially receiving an annual salary of $15,000 as it would be to furnish him with an additional dollar in after-tax salary. If a post-retirement deferred compensation arrangement were used, the cost would be only 59 per cent of the direct salary cost and, if a stock option, fully 172 per cent. The calculations follow from an analysis which is spelled out in detail in the National Bureau book, to which I refer you for a more leisurely description of the procedures.[8] In any case, the question asked is: If firms adopt various supplements to salary for their executives, how do the after-tax outlays thereby required compare with the after-tax cost of providing the *same level* of reward on a straight cash basis instead? While the results are presented for the three major supplements separately, their relationship to each other necessarily follows from their common comparison with salary costs.

Several features of the tabulations seem noteworthy. First, the 1964 tax reduction not surprisingly diminished the relative attractiveness of deferred and contingent rewards as compared with direct cash payments. With the exception of stock options at fairly low income levels, indirect remuneration now provides somewhat less of a tax shelter than before—not enough less, however, to suggest that the "swing back to cash" I have been hearing about the last few years makes much sense. Salary still is an exceedingly inefficient means of compensation.

The apparent aberration in relative stock option costs in the $15,000-$25,000 income range reflects the fact that lower ordinary tax rates also produce lower capital gains rates, and the rate profile in that range has made options marginally less *inefficient* nowadays than prior to 1964. I should perhaps point out that I have interpreted the "cost" to the employer company of a stock option as the dilution cost involved in selling marketable securities to its employees at a price below their prevailing market price. Even though no direct cash outlay is involved, the firm's shareholders do in fact suffer a diminution of their resources as compared with the inflow of funds that would have occurred had the shares been sold at full market price instead. Since this "opportunity cost" is not tax-deductible, we have a situation wherein at many salary levels additional *deductible* cash payments would involve a smaller penalty to the firm than the option creates.

In that light, we observe that other forms of supplemental compensation dominate stock options from a cost standpoint at *all*

---

[8] See *ibid.,* Appendix M, pp. 346-361.

levels of income under the 1964 Revenue Act.[9] Even under the old tax schedule, options were inferior up to base salary of $750,000 annually. It would appear, then, that the option "boondoggle" has had its seamy side even for those organizations which have been alleged to make most profitable use of the device.

The Cost of the Actual Pay Package

The tables are carried out to salary figures of $1.5 million, not because I perceive decisions on compensation to be made at that level very frequently, but in part because this phenomenon of option costs required that I go that far in order to find a case in which options *would* be the least expensive reward to provide. A more compelling reason, however, concerns the final issue I would like to raise. Given a schedule of the relative costs of different arrangements, we can turn to a determination of the extent to which the corporations in the sample studied actually were efficient in designing their observed senior executive compensation packages, first, as compared with the cost of accomplishing the same results via salary and bonus alone, and, second, as compared with the *optimum* cost package. For that purpose, we shall need the full range of the tabulations since, as noted earlier, the typical top executive in large manufacturing firms would have required a salary slightly in excess of $1.5 million annually from 1955 through 1963 to match the after-tax pay generated by all his rewards.

Table 2 summarizes the outcome of the relevant computations. Data are offered showing the cost of the actual pay package for the top executive in each firm and for the top five as a group, both under the pre-1964 and post-1964 tax schedules. Thus, it turns out that the entire range of supplemental rewards adopted in practice by large firms for their highest-paid men during the last nine years of the study were just 25 per cent as expensive in total as an equally-remunerative salary increase for the same men would have been. The observed actual salary and bonus base was taken as given, and this 25 per cent figure therefore refers only to the cost of the fringe benefits provided over and above that base.

---

[9] The tax rates used in this calculation, it should be noted, are not the calendar 1964 rates, but those which pertained from 1965 on after the two-step reduction took full effect.

TABLE 2

COST OF THE 1955-1963 LARGE MANUFACTURING CORPORATION
EXECUTIVE FRINGE BENEFIT PACKAGE IN RELATION TO THE
COST OF AN EQUIVALENT PURE SALARY PACKAGE

A. UNDER THE ACTUAL TAX SCHEDULE IN EFFECT

Group	Actual Cost as Per Cent of Pure Salary Cost	Optimum Cost as Per Cent of Pure Salary Cost	Actual Cost as Per cent of Optimum Cost
Top executives	25%	19%	132%
Top five executives	25%	15%	167%

B. UNDER THE REVENUE ACT OF 1964

Group	Actual Cost as Per Cent of Pure Salary Cost	Optimum Cost as Per Cent of Pure Salary Cost	Actual Cost as Per Cent of Optimum Cost
Top executives	64%	39%	164%
Top five executives	61%	36%	170%

By extension, of course, our conclusion in principle would be that the salary payments themselves should have been reduced and other arrangements substituted. Interestingly enough, the combined relative costs of fringe benefits vs. salary for both the top and top-five men were 25 per cent, apparently reflecting the same sort of systematic compensation tax planning process which emerged from our earlier examination of effective tax rates. We can, by the way, turn this result around and assert that firms were able to provide *four times* as much supplemental compensation as they would have been able to provide in salary at the same net cost.

The second phenomenon we observe is that the least-cost fringe benefit package (the second column in the table) would have been only 19 per cent as expensive as salary for the highest-paid men in the sample, and 15 per cent as expensive for the five highest-paid together. Actual costs were therefore 132 per cent and 167 per cent, respectively (column three), of optimum costs. Unfortunately, however, the optimum was in a practical sense unattainable, since it would have consisted almost exclusively of pension benefits. Because firms must make their retirement plans nondiscriminatory, it would not have been possible to provide pensions large enough for their upper management group to achieve the necessary levels of reward by that means alone without distorting the entire structure of benefits under the plan.[10]

It is also, of course, a good question as to whether the executives involved would really have preferred pension increases to the exclusion of all other supplemental devices. Having said this, my reaction is that firms did a reasonably good job, after all, in putting the package together. They appear to have been within striking distance of the practical cost minimum, and to have done rather well in reflecting tax considerations in their planning for different levels of reward.

The lower portion of Table 2 records the outcome of a corresponding set of calculations using post-1964 tax rates. We see that, if the 1955-1963 executive compensation package were duplicated today, the overall cost of the relevant fringe benefits would rise from 25 to slightly over 60 per cent of the cost of an equivalent salary increase. The optimum package—again consisting largely of pension promises—would be nearly 40 per cent as expensive as straight salary. Both these results clearly reflect the now-smaller tax burden on immediate cash income, but they still document an opportunity for significant cost savings through appropriate policy decisions. My expectation is that the make-up of the pay package has *not* changed drastically since 1963 and, hence, that these cost comparisons are not too unlike those which an extension of the data through 1968 would produce.

Summary

We may therefore conclude that the process of "tax minimization" as an element in compensation strategies has in fact had the intended result of both keeping overall effective rates on the personal income of the recipients quite modest and permitting firms to furnish substantial amounts of top executive remuneration at costs far below those with which they might otherwise have been confronted. Since, even so, the data on rates of growth in corporate executive pay during the last quarter-century suggest that upper management has not done as well as other professional oc-

---

[10] And perhaps exceeding the 15 per cent limit on deductible contributions to that plan by the corporation.

cupational groups nor as well as other, lower-level employees within their own firms,[11] we can infer that without the careful attention to tax factors exhibited in the figures we have discussed here, the historical record would look very poor indeed. My hope is that those figures provide some sense of the empirical dimensions of the tax reduction effort and that they cast up the features of the current-day compensation transaction in a way that will improve our understanding of the issues involved.

---

11 Lewellen, *op. cit. supra* note 1, pp. 162-180.

CHAPTER X

DISCUSSION OF TAXES AND BENEFIT PLANS
FOR EXECUTIVES

Chairman Roy A. Wentz, Jr., E. I. du Pont de Nemours & Company: We have asked two very competent people to act as our beginning questioners. We have Rick Landauer, who is a consultant with Towers, Perrin, Forster & Crosby, Inc., and Chris Branda, who is with Dechert, Price & Rhoads. We are not intending to restrict comments to these two, however. We hope to have audience participation later.

Rick, do you have some comment or question that you would like to throw at Henry Rothschild?

Mr. U. E. Landauer, Towers, Perrin, Forster & Crosby, Inc., New York: Yes. One of the major elements in executive compensation packages, which was mentioned in earlier talks, and which is certainly included in the overall programs that Henry was discussing, is, of course, company stock.

One of the questions which arises—and where I think his comments might be valuable—is the situation where the stock of the company involved is not appreciating at rates which are as attractive as they might have to be to make it a really rewarding form of compensation. Most of the areas in which stock is used get their attractiveness because of the capital gains aspect. Of course, that demands some sort of appreciation.

My question really is: What approaches are possible, or desirable, or are being used, in situations where this appreciation element is not all that it might be in the stock of a particular company?

Mr. V. Henry Rothschild, 2nd, Attorney, New York: A number of companies today have been basing deferred compensation on a portfolio of securities of other companies. This is true not only in the case of a company with stock which is not going places, but in one company, for example, the executives now have so much stock that they want to diversify. At the same time, the president is reluctant to see them sell the stock they received.

The plan that that company is considering and which has been adopted by other companies is one under which, instead of receiving, on termination of employment, cash or stock of the company, they will receive cash equivalent to the value of a portfolio of securities which has been acquired at the instance of the board of directors for the purpose of measuring compensation under the contract.

Now, I might carry this a step further and then point out the obvious questions involved, legal, tax, and otherwise.

I asume that we are all familiar with restricted stock, but just to summarize it—and incidentally, if we have time, there are many subjects which obviously I have not covered which I will be happy to comment on in case anybody wants me to—restricted stock basically is stock which is transferred immediately subject to restrictions, usually against sale during employment, and under present tax rules this stock is not taxable when transferred and when the restriction is removed through being able to sell, the tax is based on the value at the time of the transfer, or when the restrictions are removed, whichever is the less, which enables the executive to own stock until he is able to sell it.

Now, a few companies have carried this diversified portfolio concept into restricted stock. They have transferred certificates in mutual funds subject to restrictions. As you know, there is an article in *Taxes* magazine,[1] very unfriendly, I might say, to the present tax treatment of restricted stock, in which the distinguished author, Professor Blum, referred to the case of a transfer of IBM stock to the professor himself in payment of a bonus.

But, to return to the use of securities of another company, there are two questions presented which I will just mention briefly: One, how do you justify that to your stockholders? Two, what kind of an incentive is that?

---

1 Walter J. Blum, "Restricted Stock Arrangements Reconsidered," *Taxes—The Tax Magazine,* 46 (September, 1968), 598-606.

Well, we have actually had one plan in which we justified it to the stockholders and which they voted for favorably and without criticism. The basic reason we gave was a simple one: The company did not want them to sell that stock but was willing for them to diversify without having to sell their company stock in order to do so.

The other question involves unreasonableness of compensation at the time of pay-off, both for corporate and tax purposes. While the question is not free from doubt, I think that this could be held to be valid in much the same way as the phantom stock plan was held valid in the Koppers case,[2] although, as I say, there are questions.

Christopher Branda, Jr., Dechert, Price & Rhoads, Philadelphia: I wonder if I can just follow up on the same subject of discussion a little bit? Henry mentioned the restricted stock as being the seventh wonder of the world and it is true that many listed public companies seem to be using not only their own stock under restricted stock plans but also stocks of other companies, and stocks of mutual funds. In some cases the restricted stock in question is left up to the choice of the individual employee.

Now, Henry, you said that you had some doubts as to the efficacy of using anyone else's stock and complying with the regulations dealing with restricted stock. I would like to ask your comments on two aspects of that.

I think certainly restricted stock of some other corporation or of a mutual fund seems to fit within the literal language of the regulations dealing with restricted stock. I would like to know, however, whether you think that possibly this might be subject to attack by the Treasury on two grounds: first, the general ground of business purpose for imposing restrictions upon the disposition of anyone's stock other than your own, and second, whether under state law a corporation can validly place restraints on alienation on anyone's stock other than its own.

Mr. Rothschild: Well, that second question is a fascinating one. I have not considered that. Let me take up the first one, though. The regulations cover property, and I know at least one very re-

---

[2] Lieberman v. Becker, 34 Del. 490, 155 Atl. 2d 596 (1959).

sponsible firm that has taken the position, without a ruling, that the regulations justify the transfer of stock of other companies or mutual funds.

In so far as placing restrictions on the disposition of the stock, you say it could be attacked on the basis of lack of business purpose, and I agree. However, when you have a regulation that is clear on its face and its terms, I do not see why, simply because there may be a feature of getting a tax benefit with it, that you could upset it simply on that ground. I agree that where you are using a device it might be upset, but the regulation says "property."

I am not quite clear on how state law would affect putting restraints on the disposition. What is your own view on that, may I ask?

Mr. Branda: I haven't gone into this in any great degree of detail, but I have always had a feeling that the common law frowns upon restraints on alienation of property. The common situations that we think of in that area are usually ones where the person placing the restraints on alienation has some good purpose for doing so. Now, conceivably compensating one's own employees might be enough of a purpose to justify the state courts in saying that these restrictions are valid, but—

Mr. Rothschild: Couldn't you go a step further and say that you will have the stock but you will have no right to sell it unless you stay in the employ of the company for five years, at which time you will be able to sell it? There, it seems to me, you have a business purpose, you have a real direct business purpose. It doesn't have to be stock in the owned company. Secondly, don't you think the restraint on alienation there could also be justified on the ground of reasonableness of purpose that you mention?

Mr. Branda: I think that is right. In fact, there is absolutely no authority on the subject, and I would not be at all surprised if the government would seize upon this as a ground for attacking the use of stock of other companies.

Mr. Rothschild: I would like to make one more caveat here. As everyone here must realize, ever since the Dow Jones Company saw fit to publish its private ruling in *The Wall Street Journal* in August, 1967, and a revenue ruling was issued in February,

1968, and *Fortune* magazine wrote an article[3] about the wonderful world of restricted stock and the *Kiplinger Tax Letter* called attention to the fact that it is just a question of time before the rules are going to be changed, I think it is reasonable to assume from all these factors put together that a change may be in the offing.

Mr. Branda: May I just follow this up with one other question which I suppose is somewhat on the technical side: I believe some people have suggested that if stock of a mutual fund is used that perhaps the requirement—whether it is the Investment Company Act, or what, I don't know—but in any event apparently there is some rule which requires any open-end mutual fund to redeem its shares at any time, and some people have suggested that this particular requirement might in effect nullify restrictions which any corporation attempts to put on the shares of a mutual fund. Do you think there is anything to that?

Mr. Rothschild: Well, I know that that has been the position of the Internal Revenue Service unit which has been handling this particular matter. In one way or another, at least at the last reading, they have avoided issuing a ruling on any restricted stock mutual funds. They have found reasons to duck it. Now, they may have issued one. They hadn't at my last reading. Do you know of any ruling, Hy, on mutual funds transferred as restricted stock?

Mr. Herman C. Biegel, Lee, Toomey & Kent, Washington, D.C.: Not on mutual funds, but on shares of other companies, that is, a group of funds. I always seem to be the Cassandra at these sessions and, even though I put limitations on my participation in this program, I must speak a little bit about it.

I think restricted stock is fine. I think the Treasury has been most liberal in its construction of the statute. However, like every good tax device, it is soon stretched out of all context. With the variations on the theme that the ingenious tax lawyer and consultant can come up with, especially by extending it to property, other than the stock of the employer company, I think the restricted stock device is going to be pulled down. It has happened to split dollar insurance, it has happened to other forms of de-

---

[3] Jeremy Main, "An Expanding Executive Pay Package," *Fortune*, June 15, 1968, 166.

ferred compensation, and it is inevitable that if all the "smart thinking" is put on variations of this device, you can be sure that the Treasury slowly but inexorably will be after it and the device will be "out the window."

I am on the other side of a case which is pending in the Service now for the application of the restricted stock theory to a million dollars in blue chip securities—

Mr. Rothschild: What kind of securities?

Mr. Biegel: Blue chips—and they were picked by the so-called employee, or his adviser. Changes within the portfolio can be made by his adviser. The employee will get the dividends, of course, and he will have the right to vote the securities. At first the ruling was sailing blithely through the Internal Revenue Service until someone higher up saw the potential dangers. The ruling has been sitting there for one year, and if I had to take bets at this time I would say that ruling will never issue. If the Service eventually decides not to rule I would expect it to be accompanied shortly thereafter by a TIR stating, "The applicable scope of the restricted stock provisions of the Code are now much circumscribed."[4]

So, while I try to urge caution to my fellow conspirators in this field, I know it falls on deaf ears. I don't expect much that way. If I had to guess, I would say the device is going to be killed.

Chairman Wentz: Chris, would you like to start off the questions to Professor Lewellen?

Mr. Branda: Bill, there is one thing that impressed me—I think this was shown by your Table 1—and that was that even under the '64 Revenue Act you had to get up to quite a large compensation level before you found out that it would cost less to provide a pension under a qualified plan than it would to provide what I take to be ordinary deferred compensation, that is, ordinary income. To my uninitiated eye, with the tax advantages which you

---

[4] On October 26, 1968, the Internal Revenue Service issued TIR-998 which suspended the issuance of rulings involving transfers of stock or other property subject to restrictions. On the same date the Treasury Department proposed amendments to §§1.61-2 (d) (5) and 1.421-6 (d) of the Income Tax Regulations revising substantially the existing regulations dealing with the taxation of restricted stock and other property.

get in a qualified pension or profit-sharing plan, that is, the immediate deduction for the contributions plus the tax-free build-up due to the complete tax exemption of the trust on both income and capital gains, I couldn't quite understand this. Can you clear this up?

Professor Wilbur G. Lewellen, Purdue University: Well, I don't know whether I can or not. It depends on whether we talk about the new tax schedule or the old. The old schedule showed pensions to be the best all along the line except at fairly low income levels, better than deferred pay. Under the new tax schedule they are not as good as deferred compensation until about $100,000 of salary.

Maybe this is a reflection of the assumptions built into these calculations, and the calculations themselves are relatively obscure but not illogical. Differences between individual annuity premium rates and personal annuity rates favor the pension, in my eyes, as compared with the amount of salary it would take to go out and buy an equivalent individual annuity from an insurance company. It would appear as though the price of those annuities, therefore, is sufficiently high, that to take that vehicle instead would be sufficiently more expensive than the corporation's pension plan, that deferred pay would have been better. I think you have a sort of reflection of the loading charge on individual annuity premiums. These are noncontributory pensions, by the way.

Mr. Rothschild: Of course, you will notice that there is a big difference between this very scholarly paper of Professor Lewellen's and the actual case that I talked about just before his speech. I mean, one was an actual case of a principal executive of one of the 50 largest corporations, by the way. I don't know why it didn't fall within these statistics. I wish he were here; he might be able to explain.

But my basic question is: When you figure the profits, you take the option at the time—the spread at the time of exercise of option. Is that right?

Professor Lewellen: Yes.

Mr. Rothschild: Now, what about sales of stock? Do you take those into consideration?

Professor Lewellen: Bargain sales?

Mr. Rothschild: Well, I mean—at lunch hour you gave me to

understand you were considering, for income tax purposes at least, sales of stock which the executive had made.

Professor Lewellen: Well, I am not sure whether this is what you mean or not, but I valued the stock options in these data which suggest that they, like salaries, comprise one-third of total pay. Stock options for the top executives in these companies are about as important as salary, or were in 1955 through 1963, and my definition of the reward that a man gets from an option is in effect that difference between the option price and the market price at the time he purchases it, at the time the option is exercised. The cost to the company is that same price difference, so that the after-tax cost to the company is the before-tax gain to the executive.

I didn't ask, in valuing stock options, what happened after the man acquired the stock. It seems to me that that is an investment decision and the subsequent date when he decides—if he decides—to dispose of the shares has no relation to the stock option plan itself. The measure of his compensation is his ability to buy something cheap. The date when he does make that purchase is the date when I value how much he made from the stock option.

Mr. Rothschild: When you figure the cost to the company of deferred compensation, do you take into consideration the postponement of the tax deduction?

Professor Lewellen: Yes. Right.

Mr. Rothschild: How do you compute that? I mean, do you use an interest factor for the use of the money? Is that it?

Professor Lewellen: I believe, if I recall correctly, what I assumed was that the corporation could put money to work at 10 per cent after taxes a year and the executive at 5 per cent. Those assumptions do not make a great difference. I did a sensitivity analysis in the study and the results are fairly insensitive to changes in these assumptions, so I would say if the company can do better with the money than the executive can because of its internal profitable reinvestment opportunity, it is to their advantage not to pay him now but to pay him later. Similarly, because of personal tax factors, it is to his advantage not to take the money now but to take it later. But in all these there is an interest rate, a time value of money kind of adjustment, figures chosen quite arbitrarily but ones which I think—5 per cent after taxes, for example—may have looked better in the late 50's than they do now. I don't know, but that, I think, is not unreasonable as an estimate of what these men could earn after taxes.

Mr. Rothschild: One final question: You figure what the value of the pension is to the individual, based on what an individual annuity would cost. Right?

Professor Lewellen: Right.

Mr. Rothschild: How about cost to the company? Do you take that same figure?

Professor Lewellen: No, the cost to the company is that group annuity rate which it pays to an insurance company, or however it funds its plan, the amount it costs them to do a group annuity.

Mr. Rothschild: How can you estimate that? How do you get that cost factor?

Professor Lewellen: In doing this I averaged individual annuity premium rates and group annuity rates from large insurance companies. I assumed in these calculations that group annuities were 10 per cent cheaper than individual annuities, which I think is probably not too far wrong.

Chairman Wentz: Rick!

Mr. Landauer: One of the things which emerges from this discussion and from some of the things which Henry indicated earlier is that the executive compensation program is getting more complex every year. There are clear indications, at least in my experience, and I know in that of some of the others sitting here, that the degree of understanding on the part of top executives of what they have actually got may not be adequate in many cases. It may even be so inadequate that it leads to steps and actions by the executive which destroy some of the tax advantages which he gets out of the program.

I would be interested in comments on this particular point. As a matter of fact, Roy might have some comments on this, and Bill, we might put him to work here.

Chairman Wentz: I certainly do not want anybody to take anything I say as based on personal experience with Du Pont Company executives, but I have heard of situations where an executive has exercised, or tried to exercise, a stock option at a price which was in excess of the market value of the stock at the time he tried to exercise the option, which certainly doesn't indicate that he had a very good understanding of what was going on.

I would suppose that anybody dealing with a company that has a stock option plan has had to deal with a situation where, in spite of everything you have told the guy about what he has to do to obtain the benefits from a qualified stock option, he still has walked out after he has exercised that option and given that stock to his son and, boom, there go his tax advantages. This just happens. I don't know what you do about it.

I think that Professor Lewellen's studies here indicate that deferred compensation, including pensions, offers a tremendous advantage to an executive.

I wonder what the experience would be so far as adoption of these plans is concerned if in every case the determination as to whether or not compensation would be deferred was left to the individual employee. Certainly there are some plans that we know about where employees do have a right to elect to take deferred compensation as opposed to current compensation.

Mr. Rothschild: Well, as you all know, as the result of the court decision in the *Hicks* case, which was in effect not acquiesced in by the Commissioner of Internal Revenue, and subsequently of a specific revenue ruling issued in December of this past year, the Service has permitted an individual to elect between current cash —in substance between receiving a bonus currently and deferring it on a case-by-case basis. Up to that time it was the general consensus that you had to have some kind of reasonable classification —that the individual could not make the determination himself.

Now, in the revenue ruling the election was made as late as December 15 and it was held that there was no constructive receipt involved because the award was forfeitable through conditions such as noncompetition. Even before that ruling we were all pretty well satisfied, and rulings, private rulings, had been obtained, including one that I know of by Hy Biegel, that a ruling made in advance of the year would not result—a choice made in advance of the year would not result—in constructive receipt.

Addressing myself now to the specific question: How has this worked? Actually I think the real answer is it is too early to judge how many people are electing deferred compensation, because this election procedure is now being offered to a group either which was larger than those to which it had been offered before or which had been forced to take deferred compensation before, and there has not been enough experience or enough knowledge, really, to make an intelligent appraisal.

I know of one case where a plan was installed for the first time last year for 25 executives, and a choice was given as between short-term deferment and long-term deferment. It is a large company, but only 25 were involved. Actually, only 10 of the 25 highly-paid executives elected deferment, because they weren't sure as to how that deferment was going to be paid, and if you are going to pay deferred compensation solely in cash, there are two important factors to bear in mind.

One is that you cannot count that compensation toward your pension, particularly in view of the very recent ruling which indicates that a plan will be disqualified if deferred compensation is considered. Secondly, with today's rate of inflation you will be getting a dollar which is depreciating, as I indicated, at the rate of 4 per cent or more a year, so the form of payment is a very, very important factor in determining what a man is to receive.

Where the choice has been between cash and stock I think in the top group there has been a definite predilection for deferred compensation. I think that age is a very important factor here. The younger man does not want it. The man approaching retirement is interested in it.

I know that when Professor Lewellen gets at this point we will have a scholarly study on it. This is just from my practical experience at the moment. I do not think there has been enough experience, really, to judge.

Mr. Biegel: Professor Lewellen, I am not sure I understood all of this. I have trouble with figures. I can't even balance my check book, let alone follow those statistics. However, do I understand this to be your conclusion that if everyone were on a strictly cash basis and attempted to get the results that we now get under a deferred compensation package, the amounts involved would be in the magnitude that you showed? Accordingly, the effect of a completely cash system would be that there would be tremendous payments going out from the company for the purchase of these annuities which would be tax deductible. On the other side, that is, to the recipient, in order to leave him, net after taxes, with the amount that he would get in a deferred compensation arrangement, a tremendous amount would have to be paid to him, which would be subject to tax, and the government would get a substantial bite at that end. So that, in spite of the fact that we have two government representatives here who may be taking notes like crazy, the only one who is out of pocket is the government in going from a strictly cash basis to a deferred basis. Is that correct? Do I understand that correctly?

Professor Lewellen: Yes. I think that is really the conclusion. I haven't done these kinds of calculations myself, although one of our Ph.D. students at Purdue is about to do that at my instigation.

We can ask a corresponding question, which is: What is the effect on governmental tax revenues of all this? Is the process of reducing overall effective rates on compensation equivalent to making tax collections from the government's standpoint a minimum? My suspicion is that really is the case because the room to maneuver which these figures suggest is, by and large, tax savings.

Mr. Biegel: But I am correct, then, in the conclusion that it would take all that outlay on the part of the company, of which the government would get its bite, to produce on the side of the recipient a net after-taxes result comparable to what we do by way of these deferred compensation plans, so that the government would get two bites out of cash arrangement in order to produce the same net result that we now get by deferred compensation.

Professor Lewellen: There is a balancing effect. As I say, it would take $1.5 million a year for the top man in these companies, and an average of $750,000 a year for the top five—$3,750,000 about.

The tax bite works two ways. The government would suffer tax loss because now everything is deductible currently which the company pays out, but it would more than get that back on the high personal tax rate. It is not all gravy.

Mr. Biegel: It is a differential between the individual tax rate and the effective rate on the corporation.

Professor Lewellen: That's right, and the gain is just avoiding those high marginal personal rates.

Mr. Biegel: With the ceiling of 70 per cent on individuals that has been in effect, I am surprised that you got the figures so high. Wouldn't that cut into the amount of dollars you are talking about on the recipient's end?

Professor Lewellen: $1.5 million and $750,000 are numbers which apply to 1955 through 1963. They would be lower now.

Mr. Biegel: With the 70 per cent ceiling you would have had a different result. It would not have been so high.

Professor Lewellen: That's right, and that is why the costs of these items versus salary are now higher than they used to be.

Chairman Wentz: If I can inject one thing: It cost the company less to pay compensation through our dividend unit plan, the employee realized more net, and the government came out better tax-wise—and you can hardly beat that kind of a plan! I can't explain it.

Professor Lewellen: I want to make a couple of comments on the issues that have been raised.

First, speaking of a logical follow-up study to this kind of thing is to ask a question that was raised: Do executives really perceive that they are getting $211,000 after taxes a year despite the fact that my figures show that is what they are getting? Does the transaction and these numbers look the same way to the executives involved, as presumably objective and detached measures of income say they should? I don't know.

I would like to point out, however, that, as I say, the attempt through all this was to ask the question: How could the firm go about paying these individuals in straight cash as well as they are being paid by something else, and moreover paid in a form that could be a practical form they could actually adopt?

So I would suggest, for example, that you could go to these employees and say, "What do you want, salary or pension?" Give them a choice between the income values of the two and say, "We will either pay you cash right now or we will pay you something later," and permit them to make that trade-off. There is now beginning to be some tendency toward letting executives choose this.

I guess I would argue further that, since everything is on a computer nowadays, I would like to see, as part of the statement on the pay check at the end of the month, in addition to the social security taxes, and so on, "Here is what today this month's pay is worth in terms of direct salary payments, so that all these different things you are getting are really worth $20,000 this month to you even though your actual salary was only $8,000." That would be very easy to do, once the thing is programmed. So I think it is possible to bring out the data to the people involved in a way that would impress them with the extent to which the company is looking after their interests.

Mr. Biegel: Professor, there have been studies made by Mc-Kinsey & Company—George Foote, for one, has made some, and I think the company itself has done more—in which they show that there is a breaking point at which deferred compensation is not worth more to executives than current additional compensation. That comes, according to that study, at what seemed to me to be a remarkably low breaking point. Have you seen the study?

Professor Lewellen: No, I haven't, but based upon the numbers I have here I would suspect as a result that—

Mr. Biegel: You would be suspicious of them.

Professor Lewellen: Yes.

Chairman Wentz: Could we hear from some of the audience?

Mr. Stephen Weltman, Chrysler Corporation: I was wondering, Dr. Lewellen, at what point deferred compensation becomes viable? Is it in the $25,000 range, or $35,000, or at what point especially—not so much for pension-type plans as other forms or deferred compensation and perhaps stock options?

Professor Lewellen: You mean at what point it becomes less efficient than salary?

Mr. Weltman: At what point it becomes more—going up the scale—at what point it becomes more efficient.

Professor Lewellen: It is always more efficient.

Mr. Weltman: Always more, even for the under $20,000—

Professor Lewellen: The logic of that, to me anyway, is very simple. Let us assume that the company's discount rate and that of the executive are the same, so that the penalty of deferment in terms of present value is the same for both. In that case, the company could plan on either rewarding the man when he retires and taking the tax deduction then, or paying him now and taking the tax deduction currently. The advantage of waiting would be offset by the lower present value to him. Thus, the only reason for a preference would be the difference in personal tax rates from his standpoint. If his other income in retirement is expected to be so high that his effective tax rate will be higher in retirement than currently, he would prefer the money immediately. Since that seems the reverse of the normal case, deferred pay should be preferred.

Mr. Rothschild: I would like to supplement that. By "more efficient" you are talking solely in terms of cost. There are other factors bearing on deferred compensation, such as the need for current cash. You are not considering that factor. You are just thinking in terms of which is more beneficial as a matter of cost. Right?

Professor Lewellen: That is correct.

Chairman Wentz: Yes, sir?

Mr. Herbert M. Gindlin, Investors Funding Corporation of New York: Dr. Lewellen, you have not used a profit-sharing plan, it seems to me, in your study. That is a very common form. Now, on the basis of what you have come across, wouldn't a profit-sharing plan be the most efficient for lowest cost?

Professor Lewellen: I have in fact incorporated the data on profit-sharing plans in the empirical work for the National Bureau of Economic Research. Those numbers of fringe benefits versus salary I quoted include deferred pay and profit-sharing arrangements, but I think you are right. The conclusion would be that it is better than a deferred compensation plan in retirement because if you pay it in a lump sum you get capital gains tax treatment whereas these payments strung out for, say, ten years after retirement would be taxed as ordinary income.

Mr. Gindlin: Isn't it also cheaper than a pension plan in terms of cost?

Professor Lewellen: I am not sure of that. I haven't checked that out.

Mr. William Welch, Texaco, Inc.: I would like to ask a question relating to our previous conversations about restricted stock options and to Professor Lewellen's charts on the cost of the various plans to the company. It seems to me that perhaps the restricted stock option might be the most expensive plan of all to the company because it would involve an immediate outlay of cash for the stock, unless, of course, the company has treasury stock. On the other hand, it will not be able to deduct those costs until some time in the future, so it might be that this might be even more expensive than so-called paying in cash.

Professor Lewellen: I think that is right. I think the conclusions under the new forms of restricted stock plan would be almost identical to these numbers, which suggest that stock options really turn out to be the least efficient form of compensation. In many cases they are really more expensive than a straight salary payment because of this tax deduction on the cost, and even at very high income levels, they are more costly than other alternative forms of reward.

I wanted to mention, too,—and this relates back to something Professor Smith said earlier—the concern that the way we design executive pay packages is likely to have bad effects in terms of executive performance in the economy. We might be leading to kinds of decisions which are not appropriate, especially for the firm's shareholders.

But it seems to me that you can argue about whether a stock option is compensation or not. In any case, providing the executive makes some money on it, that is what I find to be compensation.

Mr. Rothschild: So does an investor make money on stock when it goes up.

Professor Lewellen: If you find a situation, which the evidence suggests is the case, where anywhere from a third to a half of an executive's total pay comes from items in which one way or another the firm's common stock is used as a means of payment—for example, a man making $200,000 a year, which is something like the case for the top executive, $80,000 to $100,000 of that in stock options, stock deferred pay, profit-sharing plans and money put aside in the firm's stock—this involves the executive very directly with the interests of the firm's shareholders, which is the kind of result that I think economists would applaud. Adam Smith would suggest that that is nice.

In addition, I think it is embarrassing for an academician to be an apologist for executive behavior, but on the other hand it seems to me the system really works pretty well the way it ought to work, not only because so much of the executive pay comes from stock-related items but because—it aroused my curiosity when I went through these proxy statements—I noticed that the executives involved very frequently have large holdings of their company's stock apart from the compensation plan.

So I went back as a next step in this process and asked the question, "How big are the capital gains and dividends which executives get at this level from pure ownership, apart from compensation, and how does that fit into their aggregate annual income?" And you get numbers that look like this ('55 through '63 again): The average per capita stockholdings for the top five men in these companies was about $2.5 million in that period. That was the market value of their holdings of their own company's stock in addition to all these items of compensation.

Now, some of those holdings came from purchase of shares acquired under option, but remember in the option transaction, I measure its value when the executive buys it. After that he is an owner and an investor.

When I checked the capital gains and dividends on these holdings, it turns out that after taxes those run to something like $500,-000 a year, so in effect I am talking about a man who earns $200,-000 in compensation, $500,000 elsewhere—a total of $700,000 annual income—of which $600,000 comes from ownership-oriented items of one kind or another. It seems to me if I were a man in that position—which I find difficult to conceive of—I would be more than casually interested in my shareholders' welfare, not because I especially like shareholders but because the things that are good for them are also good for me. I think a system which produces that result is not a system where I get too concerned about separation of ownership and management and the possible deleterious effects of that separation.

Mr. Branda: I think the question involved restricted stock and not necessarily stock options, if I am correct, so that we are dealing with a system whereby the company does get a deduction, as opposed to a qualified stock option, and the timing of the company's deduction and the employee's ordinary income is identical. I

TAXES AND BENEFIT PLANS FOR EXECUTIVES

would think that the economic result of this would depend to a large degree upon how long the restrictions last. In other words, if they last until after an executive retires, it may very well be that this is a much more efficient system of providing executive deferred compensation, on the assumption that at that point he has a sufficiently low tax rate so that the bite will not be too bad, whereas the corporation will still get its tax deduction at 48 or 52, or whatever the tax rate may then be.

Mr. Welch: Except—if I may answer—it is just that the deduction may be, say, 10 or 15 or 20 years from that time. In the meantime they have to purchase the stock immediately, and that is an immediate cash outlay.

Mr. Branda: Or perhaps issue it from authorized but unissued stock, in which event there is no cash outlay.

Mr. William J. Glading, Prudential Insurance Company of America: I would like to ask two questions with respect to restricted stock. The first question is whether the recent ruling that Mr. Rothschild referred to applies to restricted stock, or whether it might be considered to be limited to the cash form of deferred compensation.

The second question is whether the discussion that we had before with respect to property, the necessity for some kind of property being involved in a restricted stock arrangement under Revenue Ruling 421, whether this might include an arrangement under which cash could be deposited in some kind of an account with property to be purchased periodically, or whether property, some form of tangible property, has to be purchased immediately in order to make 421 work.

Mr. Rothschild: When you refer to the recent ruling, I take it you were referring to the December, 1967, ruling on elections.

Mr. Glading: No, I am referring to Revenue Ruling 454 in 1968, which came out a couple of weeks ago, the effect on qualified plans.

Specifically, what I am wondering is whether it is possible to distinguish this ruling and have it not apply to the restricted stock arrangement, which is not like the typical deferred compensation arrangement, which is a deferred tax arrangement in the form of immediate compensation with tax deferred, as I understand it.

Mr. Rothschild: Perhaps I don't understand the question. Tell me the question.

Mr. Biegel: I think I understand the question and fortunately I have gotten the answer from the Service. We raised the question with them, and the ruling is equally applicable to restricted stock as it is to any other deferred compensation arrangement. The ruling provides that if you have a deferred compensation plan the amount of deferred compensation cannot be part of your pension base for determining what benefit you get under the pension plan.

The ruling is a little ambiguous because one cannot be quite sure exactly what the basis for the ruling is because there was a prior ruling which had recognized the amount put away in qualified profit-sharing plans as part of the base for purposes of determining pension benefits. Instead of revoking that ruling, it distinguishes it. It said in the qualified profit-sharing plan there is an amount paid out, put away, and so it is certain that the base on which pensions are predicated can be determined.

I am not sure whether the rationale of Revenue Ruling 68-454 is "compensation paid" but not necessarily taxable or whether it just wants to distinguish between qualified and unqualified arrangements. But the short-line answer to you, Mr. Glading, is that the Service has advised me informally on the very question that you raised: Restricted stock, even though paid out, cannot be part of the base on which qualified plans are predicated.

Mr. Rothschild: Now I understand the question. I didn't realize you were referring to the ruling relating to not including deferred compensation in computing pensions.

You were on the same platform with me when I raised this question with Harold Swartz and I said to him, "When you pay deferred compensation with restricted stock, that is compensation and should be considered compensation." And he said, "Well, we don't consider it such."

But to my way of thinking, I think there is at least a strong argument to the effect that when you are transferring stock you are in effect transferring compensation which can be considered for purposes of a pension plan, unless you have this question of discrimination, as you indicated.

Mr. Biegel: Well, the second aspect of that ruling is deferred payment, and the other is—

Mr. Rothschild: The other is discrimination.

Mr. Biegel: Yes. But the answer on the pension trust fund covers both points and states that it is probably discriminatory, but in any event since it is not taxable income received, or income which is taxable, the Service will not regard it as part of the base.

Of course, you could make your argument, Henry, but unfortunately in the field of qualified pension and profit-sharing plans, the Internal Revenue Service is just like the Supreme Court. If they say, "No," you have got yourself a long drawn-out battle to prove yourself right, and in the meantime your client can hardly proceed with a plan which has been held not to be qualified.

Mr. Rothschild: Well, I think it might be interesting to discuss what companies are doing which have in the past considered deferred compensation for those purposes. A number of companies have treated deferred compensation for purposes of retirement plans as compensation upon which pensions can be based. The question has not arisen squarely because they simply give total compensation, including deferred compensation, to the actuary, and the actuary simply puts that total figure in his computations.

Now, what do you do? Well, a number of companies are endeavoring to make up the pension as a result of additional deferred compensation agreements outside of the pension plan.

There is one other interesting feature to this and that is whether the ruling is retroactive, so that it applies to retired employees. There are a number of employees of one company that I know of whose pension is based on deferred compensation.

It has been my position that it is not a retroactive ruling, particularly in view of the past history of the ruling. I do not know how you feel about that. So that so far as retired employees are concerned, there has not been any change.

Mr. Branda: Well, I have been puzzling over retroactivity of this thing at all, in view of the ruling that has been on the books with respect to qualified profit-sharing plans—whether a plan which up to now has based pension benefits upon nonqualified deferred compensation has not been a good plan up to now and—

Mr. Rothschild: Right. Right. That is what I say, but on the other hand you know that the Service, in the cases where private rulings have been applied for, have not issued private rulings in later years, in the past few years, on this point, so as a result there has been some jeopardy, but I think the position can be taken that it is not retroactive.

Mr. Branda: I think that is the right position, don't you?

Mr. Rothschild: Absolutely.

Another thing that some companies are doing is, in view of this discrimination question, they are offering all employees the opportunity of deferment of compensation, on the theory that that eliminates the possibility of discrimination, and I might say that there is one very important aspect to this. The obligation must be unconditional, I think, to be allowed.

In other words, if it is conditional on the rendition of consultation services or noncompetition, then I think you have a tough question, but if it is an unconditional deferred compensation obligation, then I think there are grounds for considering it. I think that if it is offered to everybody, you eliminate the nondiscrimination question, at least if lower-paid as well as highly-paid personnel accept it, and you only have left that question of payment. That is the only question left.

Mr. Glading: I want to ask whether you can transfer cash subject to restrictions with a view to investing the cash later.

Mr. Rothschild: Of course, cash is a form of property. On the other hand, there are other provisions of the Code which refer to cash or other property. I would say that you would certainly not be able to get a ruling on that question.

How do you think about that, Chris?

Mr. Branda: Oh, I would think technically, that if your employer set aside cash, you would have to have an interest in some escrow fund, or this, that, or the other thing, which would not be strictly cash, or conceivably—

Mr. Rothschild: We have had rulings on property that was transferred with the requirement that it be resold in the event the employee left the company and the cash then would be held in escrow subject to the same terms and conditions, and the Service ruled that that cash had not been constructively received and was still subject to the same rules relating to restricted stock, but this was an initial transfer of property subject to restrictions that was later transferred into cash. That was some time ago. Whether they would give that ruling now I don't know.

Mr. Branda: Okay. If you had a cash deposit in an escrow fund or anything which bore any resemblance to a trust whatsoever, and if there were any conditions at all, or forfeiture provisions on it, I would think you would have a case where the corporation would end up losing its deduction.

Chairman Wentz: Well, if you transfer cash you destroy one of what I have always understood to be the damfool reasons why Internal Revenue does not tax restricted stock immediately, and that is you can't value it. If you have got cash, you certainly know what it is worth.

Mr. Landauer: What kind of restrictions would have a significant effect on the value for tax?

Chairman Wentz: The reason for that restricted stock ruling is that they cannot value what restricted stock is worth. That certainly doesn't pertain to cash.

Mr. Biegel: Roy, more important than that, the sex appeal of restricted stock is that when you accept it, you consider it at today's value, and you hope it is going to go up in price. That is the whole point of it.

Mr. Glading: This arrangement would involve the purchase of the stock, but not the cash contribution. The cash would be put into the account which would later be used to buy stock.

Mr. Biegel: To the extent that it lies there fallow and unproductive, you lose the ability to get some appreciation. You have to wait. Whatever the period of reinvestment is, it is lost for purposes of appreciation.

Mr. Rothschild: If you are going to do that, my suggestion would be that you transfer property and then sell the property. You can always transfer property subject to restrictions and have the agreement authorize the sale and then have the cash for reinvestment or otherwise, along the lines that I indicated before. I think the cash itself would be invalid.

Mr. Adam Hess, Aetna Life & Casualty: I would like to ask Mr. Rothschild, in connection with the new ruling prohibiting the use of deferred compensation in qualified plans, what about the use, in a qualified plan for a hospital, of compensation being deferred under 403 (b), which amounts to a joint tax-sheltered annuity and qualified plan?

Mr. Rothschild: I don't know that I can answer that question. Can anybody else?

Mr. Branda: May I?

Chairman Wentz: Go ahead, Chris.

Mr. Branda: Well, I was just going to say that, as I read this ruling, it seems to be based almost purely on emotionalism, and the emotionalism is the fact that the employee concerned is not being taxed currently upon what is being put aside, whether it be in a tax-sheltered annuity or in restricted stock, or what not, so if that is the reasoning behind it—and that, as I say, is the way I read it—I would think that in your case you could not do what you want to do.

Mr. Hess: If they are willing to distinguish the '59 ruling on the basis of the qualified status of the profit-sharing plan being the key to deferral of compensation, we are being penalized for recognizing actual compensation deferred under a provision of the Code outside the qualified plan area.

Mr. Branda: That's right. There are a lot of things that you can get away with in the qualified plan area that you don't get away with in other areas.

Mr. Rothschild: That was on the ground of nondiscrimination. That would indicate there had been no discrimination.

Mr. Biegel: But, Henry, there is no nondiscrimination test in the tax-exempt section 403 annuity, so if I had to guess I would say they would rule favorably in that instance.

Mr. Rothschild: That's the point.

Mr. Biegel: I don't know. I haven't had one. I am just guessing.

President F. Cleveland Hedrick, Jr., Hedrick and Lane, Washington, D. C.: Mr. Rothschild, you gave an example of a taxable exchange of stock for convertable debentures. It was my information that you New York lawyers were giving opinions to the effect that, while that is being recognized, the installment provisions would be applied and that you didn't have to pay the tax until the debentures matured. Is that correct?

Mr. Rothschild: I mentioned that it was a capital gain and that in the first year up to 30 per cent had to be paid. That was one capital gain. Then, of course, these debentures would have to be sold to pay part of the 30 per cent. It was one of these vicious circles, but you are perfectly right, it was believed to be an installment sale and that would alleviate the burden to some extent, but not entirely.

President Hedrick: I see. I was just wondering whether you were giving the same advice.

Mr. Rothschild: Your advice is sound.

President Hedrick: I didn't say that I concurred.

Mr. Stanley Pantowich, Arthur Young & Company: Have you got a favorable ruling on the debentures to qualify as an installment sale?

Mr. Rothschild: I don't believe there had been a ruling. I think that was just an opinion that was given.

Mr. Pantowich: I have seen some opinions. Some say "yes," some say "no."

Mr. Branda: It is my understanding that the position of the Corporation Tax Branch is that they will not issue installment sale rulings where convertible debentures are involved because they can't figure out any way to value the conversion feature and they regard the value of that feature as being a payment in the year of sale.

Mr. Pantowich: I have heard informally that they will rule favorably with regard to stock and warrants, which might be the same thing. They would not rule favorably with convertible preferred, but they probably would with stock and stock warrants.

Mr. Rothschild: Of interest to you in this instance, the action was taken under opinion of counsel.

President Hedrick: On your ruling, was that just straight debentures?

Mr. Rothschild: Yes—straight debentures. However, I operate in a very narrow field. All I know is compensation and perhaps not too much about that.

Mr. C. J. Halpern, American Telephone and Telegraph Company: I have no expertise on this particular question, but one thing that I think that you have today is that if you do have a convertible debenture which you say qualifies you, what happens when you convert the debentures? If all that you have now is stock, there will be no more payments from the buyer. If you do not have stock, is that taxable?

Mr. Branda: Couldn't that be solved by saying that in effect you made a disposition of the installment obligations when you converted the debenture?

Mr. Halpern: That is where it would be kind of general theory based on what I do not know, the conversion of a convertible debenture.

Mr. Branda: I think you have an over-riding statute providing for acceleration of gain on the disposition of installment obligations. As I say, I have not studied it and I am not sure whether this would solve the problem.

Mr. Phillip Lifschultz, Montgomery Ward: I think the disposition of the installment obligation might be nonsalutary because you might have ordinary income at that point.

Mr. Branda: If the original sale qualified for capital gain treatment, I believe that disposition of the installment obligations should also result in capital gain.

PART FOUR

CONCEPTUAL PROBLEMS IN REPORT ON
PUBLIC POLICY AND PRIVATE PENSION FUNDS

"Our subject matter this morning is the 'Conceptual Problems in Report on Public Policy and Private Pension Funds.' As all of you probably know, the present guidelines of statutory provisions applicable to qualified pension and profit-sharing plans have been in effect for over 25 years, and it was not until January, 1965, that there was issued what I might call the President's Cabinet Committee Report on Public Policy and Private Pension Funds.

"This report was issued, in the words of the President, 'to establish a dialogue between people in the government and people on the outside with respect to what changes, if any, are required in the existing statutory scheme for treating these funds.'

"The President established a Task Force, which consisted of most of the people who had worked on the Cabinet report, plus representatives from the Department of Commerce and the Department of Justice, and instructed that Task Force to meet with representatives of labor and industry to determine where we go from there—if any place.

"For two years these discussions took place and at the end of that time, Mr. Stanley S. Surrey, Assistant Secretary of the Treasury, announced at several meetings—the American Pension Conference in New York for one and the Washington Pension Report

Group for another—what he called the 'building blocks,' in which he suggested three or four substantial modifications of the existing provisions applicable to pension and profit-sharing plans.

"The Yarborough and Dent bills, introduced in Congress early in 1968, set forth the provisions which the Administration was supposedly in favor of enacting as a modification of the existing provisions. We would like to discuss at this session the basic principles embodied both in those bills and in the President's Cabinet Committee Report."

—HERMAN C. BIEGEL
Attorney, Lee, Toomey & Kent, and
Chairman of the Friday Morning Session

CHAPTER XI

ARE VESTING, FUNDING, AND REINSURANCE DESIRABLE AND NECESSARY OBJECTIVES?

THOMAS R. DONAHUE
Assistant Secretary for Labor-Management Relations,
United States Department of Labor

A RECENT magazine article reported that there is an effort under way to bring back to prominence the torch songs of some years ago. I am sure that you all remember that the torch was generally ignited by some no-good man and carried by the weak-willed woman who could not wash him out of her hair.

In any era, it is some unkept article of faith that gives birth to the blues. And, my friends, if a downhearted frail tugs at your heartstrings as she wails about a faithless man, lend an ear to the cry of a guy whose great pension expectations turn out to be a cruel delusion in the later afternoon of his life. Believe me, there is a considerable body of such citizens who have already been stung by such an awakening—their letters to the Labor Department testify to that.

We share a responsibility to see to it that the chances of that happening are reduced to an absolute minimum. When a man steps down from his life's work and stands at the threshold of his "golden years" in this affluent nation of ours, he should be able to count on a certain irreducible minimum income. That must come from social security, his private retirement plan, and from any savings that he has. More and more in this country, we depend on social security and private pension plans, rather than on personal savings. Thus it is obvious, what the private source does not supply, the public source must—either in social security or in some form of state aid or welfare.

It is clear, then, that encouragement of the growth and effectiveness of private welfare and retirement plans is in the public interest.

THE PENSION BENEFIT SECURITY ACT

I think it should be equally clear that the operation of such plans, with the tremendous impact they have on the public sector, is properly the concern of government. That concern has been expressed in the introduction of the Pension Benefit Security Act.

Opponents of the bill claim that it is not needed, and that it will harm the private retirement system, which, they maintain, is doing very well without government regulation. I suggest that this bill is urgently needed and that—far from harming the private retirement system—it will help it fulfill its potential as a vital supplement to the social security system. At present, the private system, despite its more than $100 billion in assets and its annual payment of $3 billion to three million beneficiaries, falls considerably short of this goal.

A chief stumbling block is the prevalence of unduly restrictive eligibility requirements. A lesser, but still significant, cause of pension loss is lack of sufficient plan funds to pay the promised benefits to those lucky enough to escape all the pitfalls that lie along the precarious road to pension eligibility.

A mandatory minimum standard for vesting provisions would offer at least a partial remedy for loss of pensions through inability to meet stringent age and service requirements. A minimum funding standard for pension plans, together with a system of plan termination insurance, would give participants greater assurance that they receive the benefits they have qualified for.

At this point let it be clear that I did not suggest or supply the topic for this talk. For one thing, I have a simple one-word answer to the question. Secondly, I have been castigated often enough by the insurance industry representatives to have become very gunshy about the word "reinsurance," and the Department of Labor has tactfully and officially moved off to speak of "plan termination protection."

If I may seek to clarify or narrow the title, let me say that I think most of the discussion on these issues unfortunately has not revolved around the desirability of the proposals. I think most professionals will concede the desirability of vesting and those who do not are holding to an archaic view that the absence of vesting is what insures that a man will stay with the company or industry forever, and that such a man is the only one in whom the pension plan is interested.

I think the current level of funding of most responsible plans represents acknowledgement of the desirability of adequate funding. And I believe that the view that plan termination protection which will guarantee employees the benefits they expect if a plan is forced to terminate is unlikely to draw much dissent.

FOCUS OF DISCUSSION

I really wish we could keep all the discussion on the *level* of the desirability of these things, because if that was our focus, and if we could record a shared conviction that these things are desirable, then we would move on *together,* to determine how best to achieve these desirable objectives without undesirable side effects.

Unhappily, that is not true. The real focus of most of the negative debate on these proposals has been on whether these desirable objectives are really necessary. Can't we get along without them? And most of the discussion is about why we don't *need* a law to get to them. Essentially, the argumentation against these proposals gets down to statements designed to prove three things:

1. We are moving very well toward the adoption by all of reasonable vesting provisions, so why legislate them?

2. There are not many terminations of improvident plans and few people are affected by them, so why spread the cost of preventing them to all of us?

3. The proposals will destroy flexibility of pension planning.

Let me say quickly that we are moving toward universal vesting at a snail's pace, we cannot allow even a small number of improvident plans to deprive their participants of expected security, and pension plans can provide for all the flexibility they want above certain minimum standards. Let us take a look at the proposals individually.

VESTING PROVISIONS

In its 1965 report, the President's Committee on Corporate Pension Funds and Other Private Retirement and Welfare Programs, concluded as follows:

> As a matter of equity and fair treatment, an employee covered by a pension plan is entitled, after a reasonable period of service, to protection of his future retirement benefit against any termination of his employment. Without vesting, a worker displaced after long years of service is denied all of his accrued pension protection. A worker in a similar position who voluntarily changes his employment has to forfeit his right to a future pension. Both circumstances are charged with inequity.

I shall not try to impress you with the horror stories of persons who were denied their expected pension benefits because of the absence of a minimum vesting standard. Nor will I address myself at length to the desirability of vesting in terms of its impact on labor mobility, or in terms of its impact on the nation's entire approach to retirement protection.

The merits of vesting are almost universally recognized, yet it is completely absent in almost one-third of all pension plans covering nearly one-third of the participants. In many other plans, vesting is dependent upon the individual's meeting overly restrictive age, service, or other requirements.

In the decade of the 1950's, substantial progress was made by many plans toward more liberal vesting provisions. This fact has been cited by many who believe that legislation is not necessary and that vesting will become virtually universal through private action. The situation today, however, shows only a slight change over the prevalence of vesting in 1962-63. The chief improvement has been the removal of the age requirement from a number of plans, particularly in automobile manufacturing.

Opponents of this provision say there is no necessity for it and allege that their case is proven by our own Department of Labor figures. The reference is always to a May, 1968, article in the *Monthly Labor Review*. The universally cited statistic is that, between 1962-63 and 1968, increases in the number of plans with vesting provisions raised the level of such plans to 70 per cent of all plans, covering 63 per cent of all workers covered by pension plans. It sounds like a very impressive figure, but it is not. Five years ago, the comparable provisions covered 67 per cent of all plans, and 59 per cent of all workers. At this rate of growth, it will take more than 30 years before we get any kind of vesting provision in substantially all plans.

But take a look at some of the other things that are said in that same article. Certainly, 70 per cent of all plans have a vesting provision. Thirty-seven per cent of plans with deferred full vesting do not vest until the participant is over 45 years of age—a point at which most Americans will have worked nearly 25 years, and will have only 20 years more ahead of them.

Twenty-eight per cent of all the plans which have vesting, have deferred *graded* vesting. These plans cover 17 per cent of all the participants in plans with any kind of vesting. In this group *nine out of ten* of the workers covered by graded vested plans have to have 15 years or more of service, and often as much as 20 to 30 years, before they become fully vested.

Let me illustrate this point by considering 100 workers aged 25 who join a wide range of pension plans. Under plan provisions prevailing in mid-1967, if these workers remain within their plans for 10 years, only 24 of them will be vested; if they remain 15 years, only 46 of them will be vested. Only after 20 years will a majority of them have vested rights.

The vesting standard called for in the proposed legislation would require full vesting of the earned portion of regular retirement benefits after an employee has acquired 10 years of continuous service, allowing exclusion of service prior to age 25, with benefit payments beginning no later than at age 65. Such a standard would become fully operative over a 10-year period after the effective date of the act.

If this standard were in effect today, rough estimates indicate that it would begin to benefit around 10 million participants. About half of these are participants with 10 or more years of service under their plans who are not now vested. The other half are participants currently with less than 10 years' service who are expected to remain on the job until they attain 10 years' service but who, in the absence of the new standard, would not become vested at that time.

All of these employees would gain the assurance of knowing, if they should leave the scope of their plan, that their benefits would be vested. Even though these individuals are not actually terminated, they would be protected in much the same way that any of us receive protection from our insurance policies, even though our houses do not burn down or our automobiles are not involved in accidents.

An estimated 3 million of these 10 million participants, however, will receive more tangible benefits. This is the estimated number of those who, without the proposed standard, would be terminated from their current employment without receiving any pension benefits.

The cost of complying with the standard naturally will vary among plans because of differences in their current vesting provisions, in their benefit provisions, and in the characteristics of their members. Judging by the pension plans reporting under the Welfare and Pension Plans Disclosure Act, over 30 per cent of the plans would either have no increases or increases of less than 3 per cent in the plan's normal cost. About 25 per cent of the plans would probably experience a 3 to 6 per cent increase in cost. Higher cost increases would probably be incurred by the remaining plans, most of which have no vesting provision.

Differences in the cost of complying with the vesting requirements are recognized in two ways:

1. Several transition methods are included that can be used by any plan to make the cost increase as small and as gradual as possible.

2. A relief provision is included to aid plans that incur a substantial cost increase.

Is vesting necessary? Is a minimum vesting standard such as we have proposed necessary? Yes—if the private pension system is to be believable. Yes—if the private pension system wants to hold the faith and allegiance of its participants.

THE FUNDING STANDARD

It is equally necessary that we insure that the money will be available to pay the benefits for which participants become eligible. The private pension system as a whole is to be commended for its funding practices. Practically all plans fund at least their current obligations to pay benefits in the future, and most have set full funding—asset accumulations equal to accrued benefit rights—as their ultimate goal.

Our proposal in this area is designed to bring a minority of plans up to the funding standards already adopted by the majority. Is it necessary? Yes—unless we are prepared to see that minority weaken the overall successs of the nation's private pension system.

The present Internal Revenue Service funding standard requires fund accumulations to be sufficient to meet the benefits earned each year since inception of the plan to pay the interest on any unfunded past-service liabilities. This is maintained as a basic standard under the bill.

This test, however, cannot be relied upon any longer as the sole measure of funding adequacy, because it does not provide for funding of past-service costs, and thus may not lead to sufficient funding in the event of plan termination. For this reason S.3421 incorporates an additional funding standard, to measure more accurately and uniformly a plan's ability to meet its vested commitments at any point in time, and specifically in the event of termination. Such a standard would have the additional advantage of setting a firm foundation upon which a system of plan termination can be based. The proposed new standard is built around a comparison at a point in time of a plan's assets with its vested liabilities based on benefits for retirees and for those with vested rights but not yet receiving benefits.

Although available data indicate that most plans are currently funding as rapidly as the proposed standard would require, some plans might encounter difficulty in complying with the new schedule. To avoid unreasonable hardships and to provide transition procedures as in the case of the vesting standard, existing plans may elect to enter the schedule at their current funding ratio, if this is lower than the ratio specified by the new schedule based on the plan's age. In addition, beginning at that point, the plan's funding target would rise only three percentage points per year for the first five years, with the full four percentage points not required until the sixth year. New plans are not required to meet the new standard during their first five years.

Special arrangements are provided in the event of plan amendments raising benefit levels and thus increasing vested liabilities. In such cases, the plan's required funding ratio would be adjusted to take into account the magnitude of the increased vested liabilities. In addition, if the amendment increases vested liabilities by more than 25 per cent, the liabilities created by the amendment can be treated as a separate plan, for purposes of the new funding standard. As in the case of the vesting standard, plans may apply for a variance from the funding standard, if this would impose unreasonable costs or unworkable administrative arrangements.

PLAN TERMINATION PROTECTION

Under present regulations an employer has no legal obligation to pay expected pension benefits upon termination of the plan beyond those which can be provided by his previous contributions. The proposed funding standards would prove extremely helpful in assuring that in the future adequate assets will be on hand to meet a plan's vested obligations. No funding standard, however, can be expected to provide complete protection from the day of the adoption of this legislation in the event of termination, since this would require full and immediate funding of all vested benefits.

To meet the problem of insufficient assets upon termination, a system of plan termination protection is proposed. The aim of such a program would be to provide protection during the early years in the life of a plan, before it has been able to build sufficient resources to meet the 100 per cent goal. Plan termination protection would also serve the same purpose following amendments which liberalize plan benefits and which also typically require a period of time to become full-funded.

Information on plan terminations, while not complete, does indicate that significant numbers of plan participants are left without their full benefit rights. During the years 1955-65, about 4,300 pension plans terminated, involving 225,000 employees. Forty-four per cent of these terminations occurred under circumstances —financial difficulties or dissolutions of the business—where losses were likely. Currently, about 500 pension plans, involving 25,000 employees, terminate each year. The well-known experience of the Studebaker employees when that firm closed down its South Bend, Indiana, assembly plant in 1964 is only the most graphic example of what can happen when a terminating plan does not have sufficient assets to meet all vested benefits.

The proposed system of plan termination protection would build directly upon the termination funding standard. It has been developed with the aim of providing full protection for the vested rights of plan participants in the event of plan termination caused by shutdown of operations or adverse economic circumstances.

Essentially, this system is comprised of the following interrelated aspects:

1. Plans would purchase insurance to guarantee payment of vested benefits in the event of plan termination caused by shutdown of operations or adverse economic circumstances.

2. The insurance fund would fully protect vested benefits of all plans satisfying the funding standard.

3. Plans that do not meet the termination funding standard would not be permitted insurance coverage for the amount by which their assets fell short of the amounts required by the standard, but rather, in these instances, the employer would be liable for this amount.

4. Conditions under which claims against the insurance fund are honored would be carefully limited in order to maintain the integrity of the insurance fund.

Is plan termination protection necessary? No, or at least not if you are willing to write off to bad luck the perhaps 12,000 persons whose pension plans terminate each year under circumstances— financial difficulties or dissolutions of the business—where losses are likely. I don't think you are, because that, too, is part of the overall health and well-being of the private pension system.

ROLES OF LABOR AND TREASURY DEPARTMENTS

Finally, let us consider the respective roles of the Department of Labor and the Treasury Department.

It seems strange to me that wages, health and welfare plans, vacation allowances, sick disability pay, hours of work, job safety, and every other aspect of the work relationship—the work place and the recompense for work—fall within the province of the

153

Labor Department, but pension plans and their administration somehow are not the concern of the Labor Department, but solely the province of the Treasury.

This sounds doubly strange to me since, at a time when proposed vesting and funding standards were linked to changes in tax law, I generally heard from persons who were most strongly against this, who believed that the government's interest in private pensions should positively not be based on the tax provisions of the law.

Pensions are today a very important part of employee compensation. They are inextricably bound up with the "welfare of the wage earner," the promotion of which is the basic charter of the Department of Labor. Their continued vitality and their improvement will have a major effect on the work force of the nation, on the income, mobility, and security of our working people.

I think that the development of the private pension system, and the development of governmental interest in that system and concern for it, have passed far above the original level of interest which dictated a role for the Treasury Department related to a tax allowance.

Conclusion

In the present status of private pensions, in all too many cases, the pension promise shrinks to this: If you remain in good health and stay with the same company until you are 65 years old, and if the company is still in business, and if your department has not been abolished, and if you haven't been laid off for too long a period, and if there's enough money in the fund, and that money has been prudently managed, you will get a pension.

It is utterly indefensible in a society as affluent as ours that an individual's economic security in his later years should rest on such a flimsy foundation and be so endangered by such an incredible list of "ifs" and "maybes."

For my part, I am convinced, and I can only hope that I have helped you to become convinced, that vesting, funding, and plan termination protection, along the lines drawn in our proposed legislation, are not only desirable but necessary, and are not only possible but practical. These standards, far from restricting the pension system or injuring its flexibility, will simply lift it to a new plateau—one on which it will not only grow and prosper, but one on which it will deserve and have the faith and allegiance of its participants.[1]

---

[1] Editorial Note: Mr. Donahue, author of this paper, became Executive Secretary of the Service Employees International Union, AFL-CIO, CLC, January 21, 1969.

CHAPTER XII

ARE VESTING, FUNDING, AND REINSURANCE DESIRABLE AND NECESSARY OBJECTIVES?

John R. Lindquist
Attorney, McDermott, Will & Emery

THE TOPIC for our program today is "Conceptual Problems in Report on Public Policy and Private Pension Funds." As a frequent and outspoken critic of the Report on Public Policy and Private Pension Funds (hereafter referred to as "the Report"), I have mixed emotions about that title.

On the one hand, I dislike its limitations—i.e., limitation of the discussion to the vesting, funding, and reinsurance proposals contained in the Report. It is true that these proposals (or variations of them) are the major ones contained in legislation which is now pending before Congress. The Report, however, contained a number of other proposals, and all of them taken together, if adopted, could have far-reaching effects on the private pension system. Moreover, some of the proposals of the Report are being effected through administrative action. These other proposals, which are not included in the topic for today, should not be ignored simply because our attention today is being focussed on vesting, funding, and reinsurance.

On the other hand, it was a happy stroke of genius that labeled today's program as one dealing with "conceptual problems." That is the *problem* with the entire Report—it is *conceptual*, rather than based upon facts or evidence. Webster defines the word "concept" as being "something conceived in the mind" or "an *abstract* idea generalized from particular circumstances." As we shall see, the proposals which are to be discussed today can be characterized as "things conceived in the mind" or "abstract ideas generalized from particular circumstances," rather than proposals based upon fact and evidence.

I am also happy that we are going to discuss the proposals involved in today's discussions from the standpoint of whether they are both necessary and desirable. If we look at the evidence available, it seems reasonably clear to me that the vesting, funding, and reinsurance proposals of the Report are not necessary in the private pension system as we know it today. On the other hand, consideration of whether or not those proposals are desirable entails consideration of where those proposals would take the private pension system and whether or not the end result would be desirable.

Let us take a look at the arguments advanced in the Report in favor of forced vesting, funding, and reinsurance; the evidence in support of those arguments; where the adoption of those proposals would take the private pension system; and whether or not the latter would be a desirable result.

Is Forced Vesting Necessary?

The Report advances four major arguments in support of its proposal for forced vesting. Those major arguments are:

Equity Argument

1. As a matter of equity and fair treatment, an employee covered by a pension plan is entitled, after a reasonable period of service, to protection of his future retirement benefits against any termination of his employment. The Report further buttresses this argument by stating that vesting validates the concept that pension benefits represent "deferred compensation" to which the employee is entitled because of his service with his employer. The part of this major argument which deals with "equity" and "fair treatment" is a purely *subjective* argument. For example, a widow, whose husband died just before reaching retirement age and after completion of many years of service, might well argue that "equity and fair treatment" require that she, rather than a young employee who is resigning and who has worked for the same em-

ployer for only a few years, ought to be benefited by the pension plan.

It is reasonable to assume, I think, that any proposal for compulsory vesting, which falls short of full and immediate vesting, will be open to the charge of "inequity" or "unfairness" by any person who fails to qualify for such vesting. This is especially true if the equity or fairness argument is to be buttressed by the second part of this major argument—i.e., that vesting is nothing more than deferred compensation which an employee earns through his current service. Why should some employees be entitled to the benefit of their deferred compensation while others are not? If the "deferred compensation" argument is valid, then carried to its logical conclusion, all pension plans should provide for full and immediate vesting.

Is the deferred compensation argument valid? Is there any substantive difference between a promise to an employee that if he stays with the employer until retirement he will be paid a pension, and a promise to an employee that if he produces 100 units he will be paid a bonus of "x" in addition to his regular compensation? In both cases, deferred compensation, payable subject to a condition, is involved. Reduced to its essence, a proposal for compulsory vesting which falls short of full and immediate vesting, especially when buttressed by the deferred compensation argument, represents nothing more than a *subjective* view as to *who* ought to get something and under what conditions.

Special Advantages to Employer

2. The second argument advanced by the Report is that vesting provides special advantages to the employer. At the risk of sounding unduly cynical, I must say that I do not recall that employers besieged the committee members who wrote the Report with requests that employers should be compelled to provide vesting by statute. Vesting of pension benefits represents an element of cost to an employer. About the only employer who might plead with the government to increase his costs by edict would be one who was working on a cost-plus contract with the government.

The Report cites the fact that most plans provide some form of vesting, and that, therefore, employers have recognized the value of vesting. While some employers unilaterally have included vesting in their plans in order to provide some form of severance benefits for employees who leave before retirement, I believe it would be more realistic to ascribe the prevalence of vesting in private plans to two other factors: first, vesting in plans which cover large numbers of industrial workers has been decided upon through collective bargaining negotiations; second, in plans covering employees of smaller, closely-held companies, vesting has been imposed as a condition of qualification of the plan by the Internal Revenue Service.

Program for Retirement Protection Strengthened

3. The third major argument advanced by the Report in favor of forced vesting is that by making private pension benefits more widely available, the nation's entire program for retirement protection will be strengthened. The concept underlying this argument is that if vesting is required by statute, an employer's contributions under a private plan would be made available to a higher proportion of his work force. The Report recognizes that increased employer costs might result from forced vesting, but then reaches the *subjective conclusion* that if a choice must be made between higher benefits for those who remain with the employer until retirement, or lower benefits which are payable to a larger number of employees because of forced vesting, public policy dictates the latter choice.

No doubt an employee who is near retirement age, and who believes that his employer's pension plan is already inadequate as it stands, would have a different view of any proposal which would, in his judgment, make his pension even more inadequate, in order to provide for vested benefits for those who leave before retirement age and after shorter periods of service. As a practical matter, any argument that the Report's vesting proposal would strengthen the nation's retirement protection system would be equally applicable if the Report had proposed full and immediate vesting, if the Report had proposed that benefits under private plans be increased by a flat 10 per cent, or if the Report had proposed that all employers who do not now have private retirement plans should be compelled to establish them. This major argument, too, must be dismissed as a purely subjective view of *who* ought to get *what* and under what conditions.

Promotion of Free Mobility of Labor

4. The fourth major argument advanced in the Report in favor of forced vesting is that a lack of vesting in private pension plans inhibits the free mobility of labor. In my opinion, this is the one argument of the Report which, if proved, might serve as a basis for compelling vesting by statute. Classic economic theory teaches that both labor and capital should be completely mobile. When they are, competition is enhanced, resulting in the most efficient utilization of both labor and capital, and ultimately, therefore, the public is benefited.

Unfortunately, this argument is not supported by the available evidence. First, this argument implies that there is a lack of vesting in the private system. Such an implication was hardly justified, even when the Report itself was written some four or five years ago. At that time, two out of three plans, covering three out of five workers, provided vested benefits before attainment of retirement age. Some have estimated that 90 per cent of all private plans now provide vesting before attainment of retirement age. However, even if we accept the unsupported premise that there is a significant lack of vesting in private plans, there remains the question of whether or not such a lack inhibits the mobility of labor. Available studies by both private individuals and governmental agencies have indicated that other factors, such as seniority status under a labor agreement, family considerations, and attachment to the home and community, are equally great (if not greater) deterrents to labor mobility.

Finally, there is the well-established fact that employees who have completed the age and service requirements specified in the Report's proposal for vesting rarely leave their jobs voluntarily or involuntarily. Most turnover tables recognize this fact of life. In any case, where turnover occurs among employees who have completed these age and service requirements, it usually occurs among highly skilled, professional, or technical workers, or executives. The Report itself emphasizes this. Prior public policy has not been concerned with providing or protecting pension rights for highly compensated and executive employees.

Is Forced Vesting Desirable?

The proposals for forced vesting contained in the Report are admittedly innocuous at first glance. However, one must look to where the proposals would take the private pension system before deciding whether they are desirable, even though it may have been established that they are not necessary. Assume for a moment that the validity of the deferred compensation argument and the labor mobility argument in favor of forced vesting are accepted at face value. If those arguments are valid, then the following would seem to be logical outgrowths and extensions of those arguments:

1. It would be only a matter of time before compulsory full and immediate vesting would be required. First, there would be the pressure to eliminate the "inequities" that might have been caused by drawing the line short of full and immediate vesting. The political appeal of proposing to reduce the statutory period of required vesting from 10 or 15 years of service down to 5 or 10 years, finally to 0, would be irresistible. This would be especially true if the whole idea got started based on notions of "equity and fair treatment." If you doubt the basis for such a statement, consider the difference between the forced vesting which was proposed in the Report and the forced vesting which was embodied in the Pension Benefit Security Act. From the Report's concept of full vesting after 20 years of service, the Pension Benefit Security Act would take us to full vesting after 10 years. Do you see how easily it can happen?

2. If forced vesting is to be justified on the ground that labor mobility will be enhanced, does it not follow that *compulsory* uniformity of benefits also is necessary? To illustrate, assume that, by statute, all private pension benefits were required to be fully vested after 10 years of service. There still would remain the wide disparity in the amounts of those vested benefits which exists today.

Would the worker who is covered by a pension plan which provides a vested benefit of five dollars per month for each year of service leave his job in order to take the job with an employer who has a plan which provides a benefit of only two dollars per month per year of service? Probably not. The private pension system, therefore, would still inhibit his mobility. His current employer's pension plan would not ,inhibit his mobility (since he would be vested in his employer's pension benefit), but now his new employer's pension plan would inhibit his mobility.

A logical next step to cure this defect would be to require vesting of benefits in a uniform amount for all plans. At this point neither of the respective pension plans of his current employer nor his potential future employer would have any inhibiting effect on his mobility. However, forcing all employers who have private pension plans to provide uniform vested benefits under uniform rules still would not solve the problem of mobility of labor insofar as private pension benefits are concerned. What about the employers who have no private pension plans? Would employees leave an employer who has a pension plan in order to go to work for one who does not? At this point it still could be said that the private pension system was inhibiting complete mobility of labor.

What would be the solution to this problem? Obviously, all employers should be compelled to provide uniform fully vested pension benefits. At long last, the private pension system could no longer be accused of being an inhibitant to labor mobility. Need I add that when this state of affairs came about, we could hardly call the system a "private system?"

3. If what I have just visualized were to come about, (and every argument made in the Report could be used to support bringing about what I described), would not this be a magic way of removing a pressure to increase social security benefits and to raise taxes to the levels needed to support the social security system? Once the principle that all employers must provide immediate vested pensions of a uniform amount has been established and accepted, would it not be a simple matter to raise the statutory amount of such pensions from time to time in order to meet the retirement needs of the nation? Think of it—no longer would our elected officials have to increase employees' payroll taxes in order to increase their retirement benefits! If you think that is too far-fetched to be taken seriously, look at the history of our minimum wage laws. How many times has the minimum wage been increased since the Fair Labor Standards Act was passed?

Are Forced Funding and Reinsurance Necessary?

The necessity for forced funding and reinsurance depends upon what employers are going to be compelled, by statute, to provide in the way of pension benefits. If we look at the private pension system as it stands today, neither forced funding nor reinsurance is necessary. Thus:

1. The Report states that a plan may be considered fully funded if "accumulated assets at all times are at least equal to accrued liabilities." A study[1] which is believed by the authors to be based upon the largest body of data ever compiled with respect to the private pension system shows that at the end of 1966 the "benefit security ratio" for the plans included in the sample for which detailed actuarial computations were made was nearly 90 per cent if only *vested* benefits are taken into account and was about 84 per cent if all benefits accrued, whether or not vested, were taken into account.

In arriving at those figures it should be borne in mind that while only plans which had been in the process of funding for 10 or more years were considered, some of the plans which were involved in the study had been improved relatively recently before the study was made and, therefore, the funding period for the improved benefits was less than 10 years. Where the funding period was longer, the percentage increased radically. For example, where the funding period for plans was 25 years or more, accrued benefits (whether or not vested) were more than 90 per cent funded, and *vested* benefits were 97 per cent funded. Incidentally, the "benefit security ratio" was keyed to the standard of full funding which the Report adopted. I should also mention that where a plan was more than 100 per cent funded, the excess funding of that plan was not allowed to distort the averages for all plans. At the present time I believe it can be properly said that forced funding will be necessary only if increased liabilities are created by statute (such as those which might be created by a forced vesting proposal).

---

[1] Frank Griffin and Charles L. Trowbridge, *Status of Funding Under Private Pension Plans,* Homewood, Illinois, Richard D. Irwin, Inc., publication scheduled for 1969, approx. 125 p.

2. The Studebaker shutdown at South Bend, Indiana, is cited in support of reinsurance proposals. Whenever the Studebaker case is discussed, somehow or other the fact that Studebaker employees received everything that their collective bargaining agent had bargained for is ignored. Studebaker had a pension contract with the UAW and a funding commitment under that contract. Of course, Studebaker, just as other employers, had bargained increases in pension benefits on an almost triennial basis as each contract expired. Had Studebaker failed to do what it was bound to do by its contract, I am sure that when the Studebaker plant was closed, the UAW would have taken legal steps to compel Studebaker to live up to its agreement. As I understand it, this is precisely what the UAW did in connection with post-retirement life insurance for pensioners. Use of the Studebaker case as a basis for a reinsurance proposal is tantamount to saying: "Studebaker should have been compelled to provide more than it had agreed to provide. Obviously the amount which it had not agreed to provide would not be funded. Therefore, the amount which it had not agreed to provide and which was not funded should be reinsured."

Note the similarity between that analysis of the Studebaker situation and proposals for forced vesting and the coupling of such proposals with forced funding and reinsurance. The only study conducted thus far on the loss of pension benefits by employees due to plant shutdowns was conducted by the Department of Labor. This study indicated that over the 10-year period covered by the study, terminations of pension plans because of shutdowns or for other reasons affected only about one-tenth of one per cent of all people covered by private pension plans. I believe that study, incidentally, included the Studebaker case. Use of the Studebaker case to cite proposals for reinsurance surely must be characterized as a "concept," i.e., an abstract idea generalized from particular circumstances.

Are Forced Funding and Reinsurance Desirable?

In the absence of proof of the necessity for forced funding and reinsurance, and assuming that employers are not going to be compelled to provide vested benefits which they do not now provide, there remains the question of whether or not forced funding and reinsurance of existing benefits is a desirable social objective. I believe that neither of the proposals is desirable for the following reasons:

1. In order to carry out any forced funding and reinsurance scheme, actuarial assumptions employed in funding would have to be standardized. Surely it would not be proper to allow an employer who is assuming a high interest rate and a high turnover rate to maintain that he had met standards of forced funding as compared with an employer who was providing exactly the same benefits but who was assuming a low interest rate and no turnover.

2. A reinsurance program would, of necessity, require supervision of investments of all pension plans that were being reinsured. It would not be sound to permit some pension plans to gamble with their investments (secure in the knowledge that any losses would be made up by reinsurance) whereas others would invest funds more prudently. Again, if this sounds far-fetched, consider the reinsurance that is provided under FDIC. Establishment of that type of reinsurance did not stop with a mere establishment of the plan. The Federal Deposit Insurance Corporation has its own examiners and all participating banks must conform to standards of operation established by the FDIC. I think that it is safe to say that if reinsurance were to be established as a principle, we would all insist that there be uniformity in actuarial assumptions and in the kind of investments private plans could make.

3. Forced funding, accompanied by reinsurance, undoubtedly would encourage minimum funding by employers. This would be contrary to the course which employers have followed to date and which has placed the private pension system in the sound condition in which we find it today.

4. The chief strength of the private system has been its diversity in funding benefits. Competition among funding media has redounded to the benefit of the system as a whole. Forced funding and reinsurance proposals, accompanied by the inevitable standardization of actuarial methods and permissible investments, would eliminate most of this competition. This would harm the system, and, more important, would harm the beneficiaries of the system.

KEY TO PROPOSALS

In closing, I would emphasize that the key to all three of the proposals under discussion is the vesting proposal. No case can be made for funding and reinsurance unless forced vesting is adopted. The evidence shows that the private pension system, as presently constituted, is adequately funded, and there is nothing to reinsure. For this reason I suggest that those of you who are opposed to forced funding or reinsurance keep your attention centered on the vesting proposals.

CHAPTER XIII

CRITICAL ISSUES IN PENSION PLANNING

DAN M. McGILL
Wharton School of Finance and Commerce,
University of Pennsylvania

BOTH of the papers presented this morning were persuasive. They have dealt with issues that are enormously complex. Both speakers have oversimplified the issues for their own purposes, but I think it was proper for them to do so. I have devoted long hours to contemplation of these particular issues and problems. I played a role in the original deliberations of the Cabinet Committee on Corporate Pension Funds, not as a member of the Committee, but as a consultant to the President's Committee on Labor-Management Policy that was asked to review the report while it was still in provisional form. Even though that was five years ago and I have since written a number of pages on many of these topics, I have not yet made up my own mind as to the merits of the various issues involved.

At this point in the program I would simply like to try to throw some additional light on the subject in terms of factual evidence and let you make up your own minds.

FUNDING

Mr. Lindquist referred to the funding study that Frank Griffin and Charles L. Trowbridge have carried out for the Pension Research Council.[1] This is a study of all private pension plans which as of 1966 had been in process of funding for 10 years or more,

---

[1] See Chapter 12, footnote 1.

covered 25 or more employees, and qualified under Treasury regulations.

In order to broaden the base of participation and to identify subgroups of plans that might lend themselves to sampling, the data-gathering for this study was divided into two phases. The first phase sought information of a general nature that would give a clear profile of the plans under study and which could be supplied with minimum effort by the insurance companies and actuarial consulting firms that cooperated in the study. This phase, which was virtually completed by the end of 1966, produced data on 3,983 plans, in all size categories and with a full range of relevant characteristics. These plans accounted for nine million participants, about 44 per cent of the estimated group of plans in existence for 10 years or more at the time of reporting.

The second phase called for special actuarial valuations and other data that could be provided only at great expense and inconvenience to the cooperating organizations. To minimize the work and expense involved, Phase II information was sought for only a sample of the Phase I plans, rather than for all. Participating firms were asked to submit the requested information with respect to all plans covering 5,000 or more employees, one-half of the plans covering 500 to 4,999 employees, and one-fourth of the plans covering fewer than 500 employees, the plans for the sample being selected at random.

The sampling precedure followed was expected to produce a sample of 1,161 plans, when account was taken of the fact that a few firms which had supplied data for the first phase of the study had given notice that they would not be able to furnish the Phase II data. For various reasons, the special valuations could not be carried out for some of these plans, and Phase II data were eventually received for 1,047 plans, covering a total of 4,562,000 employees. The coverage of these plans amounted to approximately one-fourth of the universe. The second phase of the data-gathering was concluded by the end of 1967.

The study revealed a very impressive degree of funding. For example, assets were sufficient on the average to cover 94.4 per cent of all accrued benefits under plans whose effective funding periods were 15 years or more. In order to relate the level of funding with the period during which assets could be accumulated, Messrs. Griffin and Trowbridge worked out two benchmarks. One of the benchmarks, designed to reflect the initially mature situation, assumed current funding of normal cost and amortization of the initial supplemental cost over a 30-year period. The second benchmark, intended as a rough fit to the initially immature situation, assumed current funding of normal cost in full and amortization of the initial supplemental cost over a 40-year period. Considered in relationship to the period of funding, between 90 and 94 per cent of the plans studied had developed benefit security ratios in excess of the two benchmarks of funding progress used for illustrative purposes. If only vested benefits were considered, the funding under 98 per cent of the plans would be equal to or greater than the benchmark.

These results should be interpreted in the light of the fact that if on the average the funding under all plans conformed precisely to the benchmark, which would be a fairly normal assumption, then only 50 per cent of the plans would have a level of funding equal to or greater than the benchmark.

There were two categories of plans that were not fully represented in the survey. One consisted of plans funded through individual insurance contracts. There are technical reasons why in most cases the insurance companies were not able to provide us with information on these plans, but since they are funded on a level premium basis, there is every reason to believe that these plans are being funded in a completely satisfactory manner. One could expect that many of these plans would have a funded ratio of more than 100 per cent.

The other area of underrepresentation was collectively bargained, multi-employer plans, which generally speaking are not as well funded as singular employer plans. The usual practice with respect to multi-employer plans is to meet the normal cost plus interest on the supplemental cost, with no payments being made toward the amortization of the supplemental cost. In my view, this is not a satisfactory standard of funding. Unfortunately, these tend to be very large plans, covering a substantial percentage of the labor force. I think that all of us should be concerned about the long-run soundness of these plans.

VESTING

While our study was directed primarily to funding, we did have the foresight to make certain inquiries concerning vesting, and Messrs. Griffin and Trowbridge were able to develop some interesting figures on the extent of vesting. We cannot tell you, unfortunately, how many employees in the 1,047 plans subjected to actuarial analyses had their benefits fully or partially vested. We were able to determine, however, that 81 per cent of the accrued benefits, measured in terms of their actuarial value, were vested. This is a very significant figure, but a trifle distorted in that it reflects the disproportionate amount of benefits on the lives of older employees who would have a higher probability of meeting the vesting requirements.

This is a much brighter picture than we have been led to believe by some writers and speakers. Incidentally, I was a little bit taken back by the glibness with which Assistant Secretary Donahue presented the estimated cost of certain types of vesting provisions. He stated with great assurance that under certain types of plans vesting would add two per cent to the cost, while in other situations the increase would be six per cent, and so on. Estimates as to the cost of vesting are very treacherous, and should not be accepted without considerable documentation and information as to the specific type of plan, employee composition, and so forth. I, personally, do not attach any validity to off-the-cuff generalizations on the cost of any particular type of vesting provision; in the final analysis, a figure has validity only with reference to a particular set of facts.

PLAN TERMINATION INSURANCE

As you know, there has been a great deal of interest in the feasibility of an arrangement under which some agency, governmental or private, would guarantee or assure the payment of benefits of participants in pension plans that have terminated. Senator Hartke of Indiana has introduced a number of bills to set up such a program, and the Pension Benefit Security Act sponsored by the Labor Department contains a section dealing with a somewhat more refined system of plan termination insurance.

Two plan termination insurance programs are operating successfully at the present time. One is in Sweden, the program there having been established in 1960. It has had very few losses and is generally regarded to be accomplishing the purpose for which it was set up. The other program is in Finland. The Finnish program has the same objective as the Swedish one, but attempts to achieve its purpose in a somewhat more round-about method.

I could conceive of a plan termination program operating in this country, only if certain conditions were established. There would have to be mandatory vesting and rigid standards of funding, including a prescription of the mortality and interest assumptions to be used, the actuarial cost method to be employed, and the period of time over which the supplemental cost is to be funded. The vested benefits would have to be calculated on the basis of the accrued-benefit cost method.

I must admit that as an insurance professor I am somewhat intrigued by the notion that pension plan benefits could be insured. In a very lengthy paper on this subject which I wrote for the Joint Economic Committee of Congress, I concluded that it is technically possible to operate a sound plan termination insurance program, but only if a number of safeguards are incorporated in the program. Some of these safeguards would involve curtailment of management prerogatives that could be expected to precipitate great opposition from plan sponsors. I bow to no one in my concern for people whose pension expectations have been frustrated through inadequate financing or other reasons, but I do wonder whether the hazard is great enough yet to impose the restrictions on the private pension movement that would be necessary to make the program feasible. We must weigh the advantages of the insurance against the disadvantages of inhibiting the sound growth of private pensions.

CHAPTER XIV

VALIDITY OF PENSION EXPECTATIONS

WILLIAM T. GIBB, III
*Deputy Tax Legislative Counsel,
United States Treasury Department*

THE FIRST point that I would like to make in reaction to Mr. Lindquist's paper is that all of us here understand what is written into a pension plan and what the pension promise really is. We understand that if a plan provides for vesting after 30 years, the employee does not get a pension if he leaves his employer before completing 30 years of service.

I wonder, however, how many employees really understand the vesting situation? And even if they do, how many employees, when they start to work, are really able to evaluate just exactly what it means? How many employees are going to know whether they are going to leave in 10 years, 15 years, 20 years, 30 years?

No one can really know what the future is going to be. Life can change, and with it, jobs. If you are truthful when you say that an employee should be willing to accept what he has got in the plan, with all its conditions, what you are really saying to him is: "Do not include your pension in your financial planning. If you get your pension, that is a bonus. However, since you cannot be sure of it, make other financial plans for retirement." I am positive that no company that puts in a pension plan expects employees to act this way with respect to its plan, because this really takes away the purpose of it.

REASONING BEHIND PROPOSALS

The basic reasoning behind the vesting proposal, the funding proposal, and the plan termination proposal, sometimes referred to as reinsurance, is to remove the uncertainty and make the pension plan for employees a real thing that they can plan on.

As a side light, if it is true that an employee has no real pension expectations, I do not understand the argument in the social security integration area of those who say: "It is unconscionable to require an employer to reduce pensions, because that destroys employee expectations." It just doesn't seem to come together. I think the fact is that the employee does have expectations which should be protected.

What Proposals Could Lead To

But the major thread that I think was going through Mr. Lindquist's talk was: Not only is what has been proposed perhaps too strict, but look what it can lead to. It can lead to complete control of pension plans.

If this argument is followed to its logical extreme, we would never make any changes in any program. We would never have had the minimum wage because, logically following the same train of thought, the minimum wage could lead to standardized wages. We would never have had the other wage and hour laws— laws about paying time-and-a-half for overtime, and things like that. Logically, they could eventually lead to complete control of working hours.

Having worked in the Treasury, and having worked in the legislative process, I have the utmost faith in the ability of the private sector to protect its rights, to make its arguments known, and to stop any unwarranted extension of what might be minimum legislation to start with.

In fact, since 1942 there have been on the tax books requirements with respect to pension plans. The tax laws say that they cannot discriminate, and in the same sense of the word, that is regulation. These provisions have been there for 26 years, and nothing disastrous has happened to the private pension system.

But of major importance is the fact that I don't think that this society can really say to itself in this time of dynamic change: "We can't do anything, because of what it might lead to in the extreme far down the road."

173

Mr. Lindquist made what was to me a very interesting comparison of vesting to piecemeal work for a bonus. I think he said vesting is the same thing as if you were promised a bonus if you make 100 more widgets per hour than you made last month. I would say that the real comparison here is to say to an employee, "If you make 100 extra widgets, I will give you $100, if you stay here for 30 years," which is a different thing.

ADEQUATE PENSION FOR SOME, OR INADEQUATE FOR ALL?

In my mind, one of the really tough philosophical questions which Mr. Lindquist raised is, if your choice is between giving an adequate pension to some employees, especially older ones who are going on retirement, and giving an inadequate pension to all employees, what is the proper choice to make? He would take the first route.

All I would ask here is that if you adopt that position, is it much different from asking your younger employees to give part of their cash wages to the older employees when they get ready to retire? I think this is more or less the same thing.

INTEGRATION WITH SOCIAL SECURITY

Mr. Lindquist made a remark with respect to the social security integration matter on which I would also like to comment. It is true that the Cabinet Committee Pension Report which was issued back in January, 1965, did say that in computing how much of social security you should credit to the employer versus how much you should credit to the employee, you should allocate it 50-50, since they contribute 50-50. He contends that the current proposed regulation, which adopts this 50-50 allocation, is really doing by administrative fiat what we said in the report we would do by legislation.

All I can answer on that is that life has changed since 1965. The world has caught up with the Cabinet Committee Report. If you compute the allocation under the historical method of prior regulations, on the basis of the current facts you also come to a 50-50 split-up. In other words, whether you compute the 50-50 on the historical basis, or you compute the 50-50 on the report's philosophy, the result is the same.

174

EFFECT OF PROPOSALS ON PRIVATE PENSION SYSTEM

My last point is: I have read in recent literature that what the government is really trying to do here—with the vesting and with the funding proposals—is to take over the private pension system, or at least conform it to social security.

I would submit to you that putting in a reasonable vesting standard and a reasonable funding standard may be to operate in just the opposite way. It would seem to me that the best defense against a universal social security system that takes over the private system is a strong private pension system. In my opinion, the only way that it is possible for the private pension system to say truthfully that it is furnishing pensions, and, therefore, that social security does not have to do it, is if it is, in fact, doing so. And it can do that only if there is a reasonable measure of vesting, and if there are funds around to pay for it. If there are no funds and if there is no vesting, and employees really don't get pensions from the private pension system, then there is no defense. So it seems to me that you really have to look at the private pension system and figure out how you can strengthen it, if your goal is to keep it viable as a defense against social security.

CHAPTER XV

THE TERMINATION PROBLEM

LEONARD LESSER

General Counsel, Industrial Union Department, AFL-CIO

I AM really a little confused right now, because my function is to comment, and the last thing Bill Gibb said has almost turned me off, in terms of my support for the private pensions. Bill said that the reason for private pensions, really, is to stop the drive for an increased, adequate, improved social security system.

Mr. Lindquist did it the other way. His point was that it was all a diabolical plot on the part of unions: It is easier to improve the private pension system than it is to improve the social security system.

I am not sure where I stand, but I am still for the legislation, and I am still for an adequate social security system.

CONCEPTUAL APPROACH APPROVED

Also, I disagree with everyone else who has spoken, because I think the title of this session is a very good one. I think the conceptual approach is really the only way in which you can look at this problem. It is true that you can make a great argument: We really don't need this legislation, because, after all, nearly everybody has vesting and, Mr. Lindquist says, executives can take care of themselves. When another employer wants to woo an executive away, the latter can arrange a good deal for himself. Most people have vesting rights and, after all, there are very few plans that terminate. So what do we have to worry about?

Of course, the reverse of that is: If there are very few plans that terminate, then it costs very little to protect the people who get hurt when plans terminate. If very few persons don't have vesting, then it really doesn't cost much to put in vesting, because most individuals have it now, anyway. And if, as Dan McGill says, all these plans are 98 per cent funded and meet the test of security, well, that's great!

I am glad that I came today, although I wish it might have been years ago, since I could then have told Studebaker workers that they didn't have to worry, because Studebaker had met the bench mark that Griffin and Trowbridge set as to whether plans were secure, and because Studebaker was funding past service in 30 years. Actually, Studebaker also had vested benefits, and they were meeting that bench mark of funding in 30 years. The only trouble is that the plan terminated, and all who were below the age of 60 did not get their benefits.

Now, it is no great thing for a company to say, "Well, we met a bench mark." The trouble with all of these bench marks is the threat of termination. I asked some of the people who made this study whether they had ever known of a plan that had terminated and that had paid benefits to all the people, and the answer was "No." That is really the key to the thing.

Is Pension System a Lottery?

It seems to me that the question is: Is our pension system to be more than a lottery that pays benefits to people who are lucky enough to stay with their employers until they reach retirement age, and are also lucky enough to have employers who do not go out of business, or are fortunate enough not to lose their jobs because of automation, technological changes, product shifts, and all of the other things Mr. Lindquist talked about? The problem is that there are a lot of people who don't get pension benefits, not because they leave their companies and move on to better jobs, but just because their employers lay them off (because of closing down plants, because the whole business is terminated, or because a company is absorbed by another). These are the people whom I think we might be a little concerned about, and these are the people who, I think, could get protection under a reinsurance system.

FUNDING AND REINSURANCE

I heard at a luncheon at the Institute of Life Insurance that there is a reinsurance system, or perhaps you call it planned termination—I don't really care about names. The original Hartke Bill called it reinsurance. I might say that the original Hartke Bill did not require a funding standard; it didn't even require vesting. All it required was reinsurance, and the attack against it was "You can't have reinsurance without funding." Then the present Administration introduced a bill that provided both funding and reinsurance, and then *they* were attacked because they had included funding. You see, the real key to it is that the people who are opposing this don't want legislation. It is easier to have a plan and not worry about legislation.

But to go back, I understand that there is a reinsurance system that came out of the Model Cities Act, which, in effect, provides that insurance companies which go into ghetto areas to insure, and who suffer losses above a certain level, will receive reimbursement from a federal fund. I think that is great. I didn't hear any insurance companies objecting to it. That, in a sense, is what the provisions for planned termination or reinsurance provide. They really protect the individual.

PLANS IN EXISTENCE FOR LESS THAN 10 YEARS

The trouble with the studies is that consideration was given only to plans that were in existence for more than 10 years. Well, what about all the plans that have not been in existence for 10 years? Some studies indicate that the greater number of terminations occur in the earlier years of employers' existence, while there are others that show the opposite. The point is, as Mr. Lindquist says, every time a plan is improved, its liabilities are increased; it is in effect a new plan.

It was no consolation to say to the Studebaker employees, "Well, the plan was set up in 1955, and it is now on a 30-year funding basis. Since it is now 1968, we would have had half the money we needed—or more, I guess, with current service liability—if we hadn't improved benefits from '55 to '68." If we hadn't improved benefits, we would have had enough money to pay the original benefit—$100 including social security. The plan actually would have been over-funded, because the social security that a former Studebaker employee was receiving in 1968 was over $100.

IMPORTANT NEEDED REFORM

It does seem to me, from a conceptual point of view, that a pension system is supposed to provide reasonable security, and that reasonable security can be provided by planned termination protection. It seems to me that this is the most important needed reform. I believe someone did point out that funding and planned termination protection tie together, and they do, but funding can never meet the problem of security.

You have two problems. You have the problem of having enough money coming in to pay benefits so long as the plan stays in existence. Funding can meet that. Funding cannot meet the termination problem. I don't want to suggest that it is a diabolical thing that is done on purpose, but employers do terminate plans, it so happens, before they become fully funded. The reason, of course, is the improvement in benefits. The termination problem can never be met by funding. It must be by planned termination protection.

REINSURANCE LIKENED TO MORTGAGE INSURANCE

We have many examples. I mentioned the reinsurance for companies that go into ghetto areas. Someone mentioned federal deposit insurance. I think the best analogy is the insurance on mortgage obligations, because what you are insuring under planned termination is, not so much the assets in the fund, but the liabilities that have not been met because someone has gone out of business. That is what mortgage insurance really insures—the unmet liabilities incurred because a person can no longer make payments.

I think those are quite practical proposals. I shall not go into the details, since I am not going to be the administrator. If time permitted, however, I would indicate that I have an interest in more than concepts. I might even say that I don't agree with all the details of the proposed legislation.

CHAPTER XVI

THE ROLE OF GOVERNMENT REGULATION

Russell H. Hubbard
Consultant, Employee Benefits, General Electric Company

I, TOO, subscribe to Leonard's idea that the title of this symposium session, "Conceptual Problems," makes good sense because it does have this overview aspect. However, I do want to disabuse you of any idea that, as the last man on this string of kibitzers, I am against everything and only for the status quo.

I do not believe that John Lindquist would think that he is cast in that role, either. To demonstrate that, as part of this conceptual point of view, mention should be made of some excellent pending legislation which goes to the point of what I conceive to be the proper and primary role of government with respect to private employee benefit plans. I mention it briefly, not only because it stands on its own feet, but because it serves to amplify my interpretation of Bill Gibb's concern about the proper governmental role with private pension plans.

THE DENT BILL

Your attention is called particularly to a bill, H.R. 6498, which was reported out on September 5. This is the Dent Bill, which, in essence, provides for a federal fiduciary responsibility provision and, to the extent that existing state laws are inadequate, holds pension trustees responsible for the prudent discharge of their duties. This bill would, I think, fill a present gap. It contains other valuable tightening aspects insofar as the Federal Disclosure Act is concerned. I believe that this bill, which initially was drafted by the Labor Department, should be supported as it was reported out, even though it has some defects. I believe that it should be enacted before Congress adjourns.

You should know that there are, however, some very significant changes in the way that it was reported out of the House Labor Committee from the way in which it went in, as proposed by the Labor Department. The Labor Department proposed to delete the existing language in the law, which says, "Nothing contained in this Act shall be so construed or applied as to authorize the Secretary to regulate or interfere in the management of any employee welfare or pension plan." That is the present law, and that is the way it came out of the House. The present law would be retained. The Federal Advisory Council, management, labor, and the public unanimously felt that the Labor Department should, to be colloquial, "keep its cotton-pickin' hands off" the management of welfare and pension plans. I hope that the Congress will subscribe to the continuation of that theory.

Proper Roles of Government

This leads me, then, in this conceptual view, to the point that government has certain proper roles. As Mr. Gibb pointed out earlier, government has put in a rather considerable amount of regulation which those who are not familiar with the pension plan system may overlook. As he pointed out, regulation has been in effect since 1942. I believe this is a proper area and that these existing requirements are proper. The Disclosure Law plays a proper and useful role. This proposed fiduciary responsibility provision fills a proper gap. But these present requirements do not adversely affect the heart of the matter that we are really talking about: that is, the inner workings of the plans, and the conditions and eligibility requirements which heretofore have been considered the province of the employer, the union, or the employer and union together. This is the real issue in the question of additional regulation.

Now, pension plans are only a small part of the total employee consideration picture. You and I may think that the only thing that matters in the whole wide world is pensions, and that we should make sure that reasonable security in just the pension area is the sine qua non. I am sure, however, that Leonard Lesser would say "reasonable security in all areas," and so we try to progress with a balanced proposition, a balanced view.

RULES AND REGULATIONS

As much as we would like Utopia to come in the pension plan, or in wages and salaries, or insurance plans, or vacations and holidays, I don't think that we should necessarily pick out one plan and say, "We are going to give this a real government workout so far as the internal rules and regulations are concerned." If there are problems, all right; let's do something about them specifically. This brings me to a couple of the comments that were made by some of the speakers on the specifics of the bill, but I do want you to know that some of us are in favor of certain things, but are not in favor of certain other things.

First of all, I think it is very important to avoid polemics about Charlie's poor aunt who for some reason did not meet the conditions of the pension plan for eligibility, or who did not have six quarters of coverage in social security—and the world is tumbling down! Well, the same kind of hand-wringing applies to the vesting question. In the case of any employee benefit plan there are many conditions that have to be met, in any kind of organized arrangement, before you start paying money. Vesting of pension benefits is one of them. Twenty minutes after compulsory vesting was enacted, perhaps someone would say, "A reasonable, secure plan is one which provides survivors' benefits." Or, "How can you imagine a plan that doesn't provide disability benefits?"

Indeed, I can imagine that some might say that it would be a good idea to make sure that all employers and employees have pension plan coverage. If we are going to put in rules and regulations that prevent the orderly growth of pension plans, these really work against the best interest of employees.

COMPULSORY VESTING

Now, let's look at the specifics—vesting, first of all. One or two points should be noted in the context of Mr. Donahue's comments and one or two perhaps in connection with comments made by Mr. Lesser and John Lindquist.

I would perhaps disagree with John on one point. He indicated that he was not in favor of vesting and funding. I am taking his words somewhat out of context because he used the words "forced vesting and funding," which was not on the program. If he will delete the word "forced," I shall be able to modify it and agree with John. I am for reasonable security in terms of vesting and funding. I think both of these provisions are desirable and, to the extent that it is possible, to the extent that this is within the financial abilities and the wishes of the parties, then these two goals are desirable, but I didn't say on a forced basis. Let me explain this, only by way of illustration.

General Electric happens to have what today is called an adequate vesting provision. We vest after 10 years with no age limit, but we didn't start that way. We started on the proposition that we wanted to provide the broadest kind of pension coverage to all General Electric employees who retired. That was the first goal. So up until 1946 we had no vesting provisions. In 1946 we modified this, with a 50-year age limit and 20 years' service, and we have modified it five times since, with the suggestions, advice, and consent of our collective bargaining partners. (General Electric happens to have about 50 per cent representation, so far as bargaining units are concerned.) This was arrived at by free interchange during negotiations, whether they were unilateral or bilateral. We balanced certain interests.

I would say that perhaps compulsory vesting is of the order of magnitude that ought to be tempered with respect to other good and desirable objectives. If Congress, in its ultimate wisdom, decides to use a shotgun—then I would agree with John that we want to watch the shotgun business on vesting very closely. I would suggest that if we go back and look very carefully at the justification for and language of the shotgun approach which is contained in S. 3421 on vesting, we shall see something very interesting.

One justification has been, as Mr. Donahue said, that vesting has proceeded at a snail's pace. Unfortunately, he didn't quote from the very latest Department of Labor report, or if he did quote from it, he didn't quote from it in its entirety, because he would have noticed that vesting, so far as the negotiated single-employer plans are concerned, is up to 77 per cent coverage—the recent Bankers' Survey shows 90 per cent.

Well, when you are almost 100 per cent, two or three percentage points in a year perhaps may be considered snail's growth, and when you are down to one or two per cent and you double to four per cent, boy, that's progress! As a matter of fact, this Labor Department report says, "The strongest gains made were by multi-employer plans. The number with vesting nearly doubled in multi-employer plans." Then there is a little footnote (always look for the footnote whenever you read these things): "The prevalence of vesting in these plans is still far behind that in single-employer plans, to be specific, 26 per cent instead of 78 per cent!"

Now, if vesting is such a grand and glorious thing—and I think it is grand and glorious—then it ought to be good, not only for the General Electric employee but for the employee who happens at this particular moment to work, let us say, for the garment trade, in a *multi-employer* plan. What I am saying is that when this particular piece of legislation comes up before Congress, and legislators say, "General Electric employees and all *single-employer* plans *must* have vesting," I am going to say, "I disagree with you respectfully, for all these various reasons, but if you do decide, then let me tell you, sir, there should be no second-class treatment, there should be no discrimination between types of employees in this great country of ours"—and I may use some polemics and they will sound and be terrific. I may say, "There is no reason why we should relegate certain employees to almost 'involuntary servitude.' Why are the glorious pension vesting rights good only for single-employer plans and not multi-employer plans? Let's strike the fetters, whatever the condition!"

All I am pointing out is that this bill, which requires vesting, has a nice, big loophole through which you can drive a Mack truck (that used to be the vehicle of expression). It says, "We are going to have a special deal for the multi-employer plan." And I would say, "Nonsense. No special deals. If we are going to have it, it is going to apply to everybody."

FUNDING

The funding comments by Dan McGill were excellently expressed. I would wholeheartedly recommend that you obtain a copy of the study sponsored by the Pension Research Council,[1] which I think justifies fully the statement that Professor McGill and others have made, indicating that pension plans today are adequately funded. The need for more regulation here has not been documented.

REINSURANCE

Before turning to the last subject (reinsurance), I do feel that we should note that Tom Donahue pointed out that he was concerned that pension plan regulation was in the Treasury and that very little of it was in the Department of Labor. He cited illustrations of Department of Labor regulation of wages and hours and salaries and vacations, but this is the first time that I have heard an indication that government wants to regulate the eligibility conditions of private benefit plans.

Are you all set to be told, Mr. Employer—if you happen to be an employer—or Mr. Union Negotiator, that a reasonable, secure arrangement is to provide every employee who has had two years' service with three weeks of vacation—and that this is mandatory? Well, I don't know—there are some disturbing elements.

Lastly, I would like to quote from my friend John Lindquist when he talked about reinsurance. I think he summed up the matter pretty well when he said, "The reinsurance problem is somewhat like firing a cannon to knock a mosquito out of the sky."

---

[1] See Chapter 12, footnote 1.

CHAPTER XVII

DISCUSSION OF CONCEPTUAL PROBLEMS

Chairman Herman C. Biegel, Lee, Toomey & Kent, Washington, D. C.: This is the part of the meeting that I think all of us enjoy most. We are going to throw the floor open to discussion. May we have questions from the floor, please? Or from the panel, for that matter.

Mr. Ray M. Peterson, Consultant, Port Washington, N. Y.: I want to speak of another dimension in this whole question and, as a preliminary to my question, I would like to recite briefly, as I understand it, the history of the authority for regulating pensions.

In the "Cabinet Committee Report" I think the entire pitch was on tax, preferential tax, the tax approach. That was one of the bases of the authority for regulation. Then came the Javits Bill, and that relied entirely on the "commerce clause." Then came Senate Bill S. 3421 and, here, the commerce clause comes first and "preferential taxation" takes a back seat. Now, there was a Supreme Court decision on June 11 that declared that the minimum wage laws apply to employees of state and municipal organizations, under the commerce clause.

So my question is: Having heard today about this sleeping giant of plans covering state and municipal employees—a growth industry—under the commerce clause, and for the same reasons, why shouldn't compulsory vesting, at least, apply equally to these plans of state and municipal employees?

I would like to ask Bill Gibb first, whether I am correct in stating the basis of federal regulatory authority, and second, as a matter of concept or public policy, whether, in all honesty, he should not be concerned with *all* employer-instituted plans, public and private, not even excluding the Civil Service Retirement System, for that matter?

Mr. William T. Gibb, III, United States Treasury Department: Let me take the comment first and then the question. It seems to me that the promise of the federal government in respect to the Civil Service Retirement System has to be as good as its promise with respect to the dollar. And funding involves dollars.

On the first question about whether you should make the vesting provisions apply to state and local plans, I think that there are many of the same policy issues involved.

The only way really to answer you is that we have to look into this a lot more, however, because there is the whole question of federal/state relations which must be considered. We really have not developed policy on this yet.

Mr. John R. Lindquist, McDermott, Will & Emery, Chicago: I would like to direct myself to the answer Bill just gave because I think the real answer to that one is that in the Pension Benefits Security Act, especially the funding requirements of it, if you did not only require multi-employer negotiated cents-per-hour plans but state and municipal systems to be adequately funded, you would not pass the bill.

I think I can speak with reasonable authority about the state of Illinois. One of my partners is a member of the Illinois Public Pension Laws Commission. A lot of people are devoting a lot of hard work toward getting some reasonable degree of funding of the hundreds of various state and municipal systems and the only thing we have found so far is that they are vastly, vastly underfunded. If you were to make these things compulsory for the state and municipal systems, I rather suspect that the uproar that would be created by it would mean that the bill would not be passed.

Mr. Leonard Lesser, Industrial Union Department, AFL-CIO: I would like to go back for a minute, if I may, to concepts. I am not arguing against funding multi-employer plans or any other plans, but again let me ask: What are you trying to do by funding?

You don't want to accumulate money just for the sake of accumulation. We went through this whole thing in the social security system, too, and I remember all the studies made. I know Mr. Peterson knows them.

The social security system is completely unfunded, sure! If it terminates, we don't have enough money in there to pay the benefits, but we assume that the United States government is going to continue in business, that social security is going to continue. If it doesn't, it's true you won't get your social security benefits, but maybe if social security just put the dollars aside you wouldn't get your social security benefits anyway if the United States government terminated. So let's not go overboard in thinking of funding, just accumulating money for the sake of accumulation. I am for funding and this is why, when I talked about it, I said that funding and termination have to be tied together.

Now, when you look at multi-employer plans, they are somewhat different—and again I am not arguing against the funding requirement. When a single employer goes out of business, the only place an employee covered by that plan can look for his protection is the fund of that single employer. When a single employer who is covered by an industry-wide fund goes out of business, under the ones I know, his employees will still get their benefits from the industry fund and the contributions made by the other members to that fund. So to that extent, there is a difference.

I think it is important to consider those differences when you are considering the problem, and that is why I think there may be some distinctions between a federal system and possibly even between some state systems. Although, again, it would not disturb me to see requirements applied to them, but at least look at what we are talking about in terms of the objectives of what a funding, a vesting, or a termination provision is.

Mrs. Janet K. Messing, Herbert H. Lehman College of the City University of New York: Should there not be full and fair disclosure for the employees, so that everybody knows what plan he is under? Talk about the tax-shelter annuity is something that I am very much concerned with, because we in the city of New York did not have the tax-shelter annuity that employees of other colleges in the state have.

It seems that there are many areas that should be taken into consideration here, and I would like to see the door open, although I realize that nobody has replied yet to the question of what is happening to the various funds. Even within the city of New York at the moment there is a vying of interest. Some groups have vesting at one point, some at another point, and the door is just wide open for a wild scramble.

Professor Dan M. McGill, University of Pennsylvania: I am pleased to report that the Pension Research Council does have a study of public retirement systems under way. Wendell Milliman, of Milliman & Robinson, consulting firm, is the author of this study and we certainly have every intention of looking into these matters. I might say that I regard the lack of funding in the typical state and local plans, particularly local plans, as one of the serious problems in the whole pension area.

The city of Philadelphia, for example, has an unfunded accrued liability of about $400 million, and a record court decision has ordered the city to start setting aside $60 million a year to meet its obligations. The period over which the unfunded liability is to be amortized is very long—80 years, I believe—but it still means an increase in the city's wage tax to three per cent, which is encountering a great deal of resistance.

I know the conventional answer to this is, "Rely upon the taxing power. You don't need funding." But I am beginning to wonder—in fact I have wondered for several years—whether, at the local level particularly, the taxing power can be substituted for adequate funding. There is a limit to the extent to which the current generation of workers will bear increased taxes to meet the benefits of retired people.

Mr. Russell H. Hubbard, General Electric Company: Just a very quick comment. I could not agree more with the previous speaker from the floor because to me this is the one area where we have a little better job to do. Whether it is in terms of public employees or private employees, I am sure that a great majority of us are in favor of the most complete, reasonably constructive disclosure and that, of course, is the objective of the Federal Disclosure Law. If the employees cannot read the printed booklets and understand them, there is no meaningful disclosure. This can apply to many plans including perhaps even our General Electric pension plan. Fortunately there are a couple of experts in the au-

dience here who know more about pension plan design than I do
—but sometimes this disclosure business takes four Philadelphia
lawyers, to find the vesting provisions, etc. This can be very complicated.

Many pension plans, for example, tend to be complicated, and it
would be helpful if they had some kind of a key section, at least
so far as the Disclosure Act is concerned, identifying where in
each plan one can find a particular pertinent provision to the extent it can be readily identified.

I also want to add two points to Leonard's earlier comments.
The first is that I think there is a difference between the funding
of the multi-employer plan and the single-employer plan. Unfortunately the multi-employer plans apparently are very reluctant to divulge information as to the extent of their funding. This
seems to be the information that we get rather indirectly from the
Pension Research Council study—that the multi-employer plans
want to keep this information close to the vest. So we are unable to
secure very much information as to the extent of the adequacy of
funding of the multi-employer plans.

The second and main point on vesting is: This particular bill
has a special exemption, a special rule for multi-employers with
respect to vesting, not funding. There is a permanent variation
provision so they can do what they want to.

Mr. Gibb: You might be interested in the thought processes that
we went through when we drew up that special provision for
vesting for multi-employer plans. The argument was made that
by employees being able to move from company to company within the covered group, the multi-employer plan was in effect giving
vesting from day one with respect to anyone who stays in the
group. In that respect it would have more than the vesting that
General Electric would be required to have and would, consequently, have more costs. The question then arose as to whether
those plans should perhaps receive credit for the added vesting
protection if a substantial number of people stay within the group.

Now, the provision he is talking about would allow multi-employer plans to come in and ask for relief from the 10-year vesting
if they can show that a substantial number of their participants do
not in fact leave the scope of the plan. There is a ceiling on all of

that which would say, "No mater what you show us, you can't get anything more liberal than 15-year vesting." So that is the background of that provision.

Mr. George K. Dunn, Zenith Radio Corporation: I would be interested in any evaluation you might care to make about the possibility of legislation.

Chairman Biegel: Well, I think we can get several views of that. Bill, would you give us yours?

Mr. Gibb: Are you talking about immediate or long-term?

Mr. Dunn: At any time.

Mr. Gibb: At this session, if I had to guess I would say no.

Chairman Biegel: No chance, you think?

Mr. Gibb: No. As for the long-term, about all that I can say is I hope so.

Mr. Lesser: I would say that obviously the bill is not going to pass at this session. I think there is a very good chance that legislation in this area will pass but, you know, you can't predict Congresses. I think, however, that it will happen and it will happen in the near future. Whether the legislation is exactly in the form of this bill, I am not sure, but I think it will happen.

Mr. Peterson: I just have a quickie comment. Under the Civil Service Retirement Plan, as it happens, the person who leaves federal employment after five years gets vested benefits that have a value that is *less* than the value of the contributions he has made. I have this information from Bob Myers, Chief Actuary of the Social Security Administration.

Mr. Hubbard: I would just note again the asterisk on Bill Gibb's reply with respect to vesting in the multi-employer plan and that is: "Make sure that the fellow stays in the group." Now, the group (without mandatory vesting) can be far, far smaller than General Electric (with mandatory vesting) or far smaller than most single-employer plans. It can be a regional plan, only in a very small region (say Manhattan), and furthermore, the vesting exceptions can be made endlessly on a "temporary" basis because the law only says in effect: "You can only provide *permanent* variation on a 15-year basis." So, are the chains of nonvesting any less golden, whether it be a large or a small group?

Mrs. Janet L. Hoffman, Baltimore City Council Fiscal Adviser:
I am wondering about the implications of future extensions of federal controls over local government employees. Such controls might conceivably affect the nature of pension and other compensation agreements. Under current circumstances the localities are being subjected to employee pressures and the necessity to engage in labor negotiations for which there has been little historical precedent. The implications for the governmental employers and for the affected employee groups may have wide significance for the private sector of the economy. Neither the public employers nor their workers have much sophistication in this complicated field of negotiation.

It occurs to me that the federal departments with general supervision over the subjects of such negotiations may be relatively neutral in the present context. Some years ago the localities would have rejected any supervision by such federal agencies on the basis of possible violation of local sovereignty. Now, they might welcome such supervision. I would like you to comment on this.

Mr. Lesser: What Mrs. Hoffman is really saying is that the shotgun of federal regulation may be less than the shotgun of the union.

Chairman Biegel: What a terrible admission!

Mr. Lesser: Which leads me to a comment that I thought of when Russ was talking about how all this was done and it was done without shotguns. It is just amazing how really no industrial workers were covered under private pension plans until the court said that that was a proper subject for collective bargaining, so maybe there were some shotguns, excepting, I know, G.E.

Mr. Hubbard: Just a moment. We have had a pension plan since 1912—before we even heard of a union.

Mr. Lesser: That's right, but lots of changes were made with the union activity. The point is that there are always shotguns, or whatever you call it. But I don't think that you can blame it all on pressures. I think that some of the things that are happening in the municipal plans as a result of the pressures may not be solved by regulation. Actually in certain areas municipal plans did go rather haywire on their own.

Mr. Lindquist: The only comment I would like to make in response to that observation from the floor is that first of all, we are seeing a great deal of activity and organization among municipal employees, in teacher groups especially, in my part of the country, but the problem here is that they feel they have been left behind already in the direct salary area. Most of the noise that is being made is: "We are not being paid what we ought to be paid. We haven't kept up with industry." That in itself is causing all this conflict.

Think how that conflict would be aggravated if we had legislation that told the states and the municipal groups that not only must you bargain with these people and not only will you reach your agreements about what they are going to get in their pay envelopes, but in addition you are going to have to fund all these unfunded liabilities that have been created over many, many years. If you think we have got trouble now, think of the trouble we shall have.

I am talking about the taxpayers' concept, people just saying, "I won't pay it." You are going to aggravate the problem if you extend this to the municipal groups, so I suspect that when the proposal, if it is ever made, that the Pension Benefits Security Act be broadened to embrace state and municipal pension plans—I am sure that when the facts become known—there will be such opposition from municipal and state groups that you will not be able to get it passed, because they probably will not get any increases in pay for the next 30 years if we are going to start funding the pensions that have been promised for the past 30 years.

Mr. William H. Welch, Texaco, Inc.: We have had a few comments about the additional cost that might be involved. I am wondering if it would be in order to ask the panelists if they have some additional comments about what the costs might be that would be involved in some of these proposals.

Mr. Lindquist: I can make a very generalized comment just by deducing from what we have already heard here today. We have heard that there is about $100 billion of assets in these funds right now. We have also heard evidence to the effect that they are substantially funded to date—not substantially overfunded, but they are substantially funded. We have also heard the private pension system described as, "If you come to work, and if you stay until retirement, if you don't die and if there is enough money . . ." and so on, that is, all the conditions.

Now, what we are talking about is removing those conditions. We heard some talk about a group of 100 employees starting out at age 25 and how many of them would be there by age 40. Just put your imagination to work, granting that, say, 60 or 70 will not be there by the time they reach 40 anyway, and that they are younger. Just put your imagination to work and think about what we might need if we had full and immediate vesting, which I think, as I tried to say earlier, I think we shall get to.

We have already got $100 billion. What do we need? $300 billion, to do this job? Is it possible that the reason we have something called transitional provisions, the fact that if you threw this thing in tomorrow—full and immediate vesting, I am talking about—the costs for most private pension plans would soar?

Professor McGill: The cost of introducing vesting is directly related to the turnover among the employee group, but it is a little more complicated than that. Say you introduce 10-year vesting, you first have to calculate the percentage of the current group of employees who will be with you for 10 years. Then you have to make a further calculation to determine what percentage of the group who have remained with you for 10 years will leave before retirement. If they do not leave, the vesting is not going to cost you any money. They would be with you anyway. Most people stop with the first concept and only try to determine how many will remain in service until the required period of service has been completed.

You absolutely cannot generalize on the cost of vesting. You must relate it to the specific facts of the case, to the age, sex, and service composition of the group. I think the cost of a 10-year vesting provision could range as low as 5 per cent of normal cost to as high as 50 per cent. Full and immediate vesting would be almost prohibitive. That is not what the present legislation is talking about. Twenty-year vesting would, in the typical case, cost very, very little. Ten-year vesting obviously would be more expensive, but it is very dangerous to mention any percentage that one might find in the typical case.

Mr. Lesser: I would like to say that I agree entirely with what

Dan said. Obviously, it depends on the plan. I think, also, one of the keys is that you have to look at the assumptions on turnover that are now being made when you talk about additional costs. I think if you look at assumptions you will probably find you can get this on the C-2 forms—that there may be very little turnover expected after 10 years of service.

There is one other thing, too, which has to be kept in mind—the cost also depends on what your funding requirements are. If you don't amortize past service, your costs are much less, so you have to, in a sense, take the two of them together.

Now, I made an estimate before the Ways and Means Committee. I think it was about 1959, one of the first panels. At that point I said, on the basis of our actuaries' estimate, that we estimated about an average of 5 per cent. I agree, however, with Dan—you have to look at the difference.

Let me make one point. We talked about transition periods and somebody talked about wishes of the parties. I would like to throw out another idea on transition. I think, as somebody pointed out, when most plans started they did not put in vesting. Russ mentioned the G.E. plan. I was involved in the negotiation of the Ford plan back in 1950. We did not put in vesting, but not because we did not know that vesting was a good thing. We did not even ask for it in our negotiations, because we knew we had a limited amount of money, and we did want to spend it for the people who had not been able to retire, who were sitting there waiting for a retirement program, and we wanted to give as much benefit to those people as possible.

I think that was right, but at a certain point when you are beginning to put more and more money into a pension plan, the real issue then is, do you raise your benefits above whatever levels you have set and say, "Well, we will just give great big benefits to the people who were fortunate enough to stay"? Or do you spend that excess money to see that all people who were there 10 years or more get a benefit? I am not for spreading out the money so everybody gets inadequate benefits, but when you reach a certain level, then it seems to me vesting should be required. The transitional period might be, in those plans that plead poor mouth, that if the benefits provided by the plan are below a certain level related to the wages of the individual, then maybe you do not need vesting, but before you raise benefits above that level, then you ought to put in vesting.

Mr. Stephen F. Weltman, Chrysler Corporation: I would like to ask Bill Gibb what is the justification for reducing the 117 per cent offset to 75 per cent. Is that tied to the 50 per cent?

Mr. Gibb: That just comes as an adjunct of the reduction from 37.5 per cent to 30 per cent in the integration percentage. Does it go down to 83 or 75 per cent, Dan?

Mr. Daniel I. Halperin, United States Treasury Department: Well, 75 per cent is one-half of the 150 per cent and the reduction comes from making it one-half rather than 78 per cent. The way you get 83 per cent is the same way you got from 27 to 30, by increasing the limit to account for future increases in the Social Security Act. The assumption would be that 83 per cent of current social security is likely to be no greater than 75 per cent of what the future social security is going to be.

Mr. Peterson: How did the Treasury Department arrive at this 150 per cent, when actually—

Mr. Gibb: Let me tell you. The way that we got to the value of social security used in constructing the integration rate was by taking the primary social security benefit as a percentage of the wage base on which social security is paid and by adding to it the ancillary benefits, things like wives' benefits and survivors' benefits, and then dividing the overall percentage between the employer and employee.

In getting from the primary social security benefit to the whole package we took a 50 per cent factor. We said that for every dollar of primary benefit, social security pays out 50 cents of ancillary benefits.

We got that 50 per cent from two places, or from two factors. First of all, this is what social security projects as the relationship between the primary benefit and the ancillary benefit; and second, this is in fact the pay-out experience of the social security trust fund, using our definition of ancillary benefits. The actual differences in opinion have been over what we would consider to be an ancillary benefit and what someone else might consider to be an ancillary benefit. As I understand, the main controversy as to ancillary benefits is: How do you treat the wife's benefit?

Mr. Peterson: My question was, are you going to *publish* the method of computing?

Mr. Gibb: You can find it by looking in the 1967 Social Security Legislative Committee Report. They have got the cost figures there—the level premium cost figures.

Mr. Laurence M. Maloney, Marsh & McLennan, Inc., New York: I have been in charge of research and I have been making all sorts of collections on comments made by companies and consulting actuaries, but my question has to do with something which was not in the proposed regulations, and that is on this cost of living. In an integrated plan, if you decide to increase benefits, you are still stuck with the limitations which existed previously. Did the Treasury even consider making a special exception for having some sort of a cost-of-living adjustment on integrated plans after retirement without complying with the mathematical rule?

Mr. Gibb: Let me just comment on it. The proposed regulations make no change from the existing mimeograph with respect to the treatment of variable annuities and cost-of-living allowances under integrated plans. They say you cannot have it, as I understand this.

Dan, I don't mean to preempt your time. Is that correct?

Mr. Halperin: Do you mean something that starts and becomes variable when paid?

Mr. Maloney: No, this is after retirement. In other words, a man would not have cost-of-living adjustment to a variable annuity prior to retirement. Now, is it contemplated putting one in after retirement?

Mr. Gibb: Is it when the employee reaches retirement, that you switch from the fixed annuity? Do you take the pot of money which has been computed under the fixed annuity method and put it into a variable annuity?

Mr. Maloney: No, this was just not to say you put in, you know, a cost of living that would appreciate year by year, but just—I know in one particular case they wanted to just make an immediate adjustment, and this was the problem which we were confronted with.

Mr. Halperin: As I understand the position of the Internal Revenue Service on that, it is that a variable annuity after retirement will be acceptable. I think a cost-of-living escalator is a different story and poses more serious problems, but this is something I suspect that a study will be submitted on.

Mr. Hubbard: I would like to ask a question. Questions on the proposed regulation have been asked by countless numbers of people who are lawyers, actuaries, accountants, students, insurance companies, and corporate managers. It goes back to the first IRS announcement in 1966. Over this period there seems to have been no penetration whatsoever with IRS with respect to the argumentation that has been made by all these experts questioning the whole mathematical approach as well as the voluminous, difficult, complex set of rules that we now find ourselves in. I just wonder, does the Treasury feel that the only way to get out of this morass of complexity and confusion is for the "unwashed" to go to Congress?

Chairman Biegel: Could you elucidate just what you are asking on this, what aspects you are talking about?

Mr. Hubbard: Yes. I didn't bring the IRS proposal here, but if anybody has a copy he might just hold it up and then you would be able to see what I am referring to. I am under the impression, from some of the folks who have commented indirectly and directly to the Council on Employees Benefits, that they found the whole package confusing, complicated, not understandable, and they made the comment that it was going to be extremely difficult in the future for private plans to continue on an integrated basis. I just wondered whether any of this theory, or comment, has filtered into the Treasury Department in such a fashion that they would care to comment as to the possibilities of a more simplified approach, not necessarily a different result, but just a more simplified approach.

Mr. Gibb: Maybe the basic way to answer is first in a general way, I certainly hope that the comments have infiltrated Dan's and my brains. We tried to have them infiltrate.

You pointed out that the regulation and ruling are long; but length itself really does not mean complexity. There is an infinite variety of pension plans for which rules were requested—and provided.

In concept and in detail there is no significant change from what has been going on in the past, except in one area, and that is the wage base at which you integrate. In the past the rules have been that when they raised the social security wage base, for example, from $4,200 to $4,800, you could integrate an excess plan for both past and future service at 37.5 per cent over $4,800.

The proposed regulation changed that particular concept on the basis that the actual wage base increases gradually and reaches $7,800 only for the employee who is now very young. An employee retiring next year is going to receive social security benefits, not based on $7,800, but based on $5,000, because the size of the social security benefit is a function of the amount of his wages that were covered by social security, and that in turn is a function of how many years he has worked under the new higher wage base.

We followed that concept and said, "If the guy retiring next year is going to receive social security on wages only up to $5,000, it looks theoretically equitable to say that the employer should get credit only for providing social security on wages up to $5,000." A guy who retires in the year 2006 will get social security computed as a percentage of $7,800 because that is the average of the wages covered by social security. What the regulation says, therefore, is that you are going to have a different integration level for each age employee.

We have received an awful lot of comment about this change. Usually the comments start by saying, "This is unduly complex. No one in his right mind can understand it and we just can't integrate." It seems that this claim of complexity evolved from two sources:

Number one is the idea that no one understands this aspect of social security, that social security benefits are paid on a sliding wage base depending on how long you have been under social security and under the new high wage base, and that it is almost impossible to explain it to anybody.

The second comment we have gotten in this respect is that, while the theory of integration may allow an employer to differentiate between employees on this basis, it is a matter of employee relations. We cannot take two employees earning the same salary but with different ages and tell them they are going to get different pensions.

What the employers are saying is, "We need most of all one figure that we can tell employees." It is not clear in my mind how, if you take a figure under $7,800, you can explain that to them, either.

Chairman Biegel: John, do you want to comment?

Mr. Lindquist: Bill knows my argument on this. I made it a couple of weeks ago, but I think in answer to the question "Can it be made simpler?" we ought to go back to first principles. I am not talking about Mimeograph 6641; I am talking about 5539, where I don't think any concern was given to who contributes what. I think we kind of slide by this 50-50 thing. If it works out mathematically we could make it 60-40 or 20-80 and it would come out the same way, if we simply want to get an answer. But the Code itself says—we are talking about discrimination and qualifying plans—that plans cannot be discriminatory in contributions or benefits. Social security is a fixed-benefit pension plan.

If I were setting up a plan today, quite apart from social security, there clearly would be discrimination as to contributions. In my plan the people who are older, who are going to get exactly the same benefits, would have to have a bigger contribution made for them. In that area for years—and I hope they never change it —the Treasury Department has always said, "This is not the kind of a discrimination with which we are concerned." Now, if social security is only a fixed-benefit pension plan, why don't we make it simple? Look at the benefit that you are providing under social security and forget who is providing what portion of it. In the first place, it would be consistent with the law; in the second place, it would be consistent with the way you treat a pension plan which is not integrated with social security; and thirdly, what we are trying to find is whether a plan which is integrated is discriminatory anyway, and I think we tend—

Bill, if you will excuse me, I think we tend to get ourselves too involved. You get the table because you are following what you originally had. Now, if you take your $5,000-a-year man today, he is still essentially getting a pension, a social security based on what he earned. The man who retires eight years from now is going to get social security based on what he earned, and that social security will be a higher dollar amount, but it will be approximately the same percentage of his covered compensation as that of the man who retires next year or the man who retires in 2004. So you could simplify it greatly by picking some percentage and say, "This is what social security is worth," and if you want to build on that, go ahead and build, instead of having this table that has all these complicated rules, because in point of fact I think it has been demonstrated—this has been lost sight of, too—that what we have got in the proposed revised regulations is a lot worse than in Announcement 66-58. With the holler that went up about 66-58, I am surprised that more people haven't hollered about the proposed revised regulations, which I think are tougher.

Mr. Maloney: May I just give you a little insight, because we have actuaries who are also lawyers and we have got two persons who agree about these regulations, who say, "I thought they were great." And this I have found not only in our firm but in other actuarial consulting firms. Not only do we have this problem with this new concept of compensation, which is the new rule, and this so-called modified grandfather clause, but one of the main things—just talking to one of our clients, he said, "Give me a percentage. What is our percentage? Before, it was this percentage, and now what is it doing?" The question comes up, what is the new percentage? We figured it, and I think it came out to about 20 per cent of the excess over $7,800, and that is actually what we are talking to when we are talking to a client.

Unidentified Voice: Nineteen per cent!

Mr. Gibb: That is when you are talking in terms of a plan that is going to integrate over $7,800?

Mr. Maloney: A brand new plan. We have one actuary who is close to retirement, and he agrees that it is complex, and if it is complex to an actuary and a lawyer, you can imagine what it is to the client. If the purpose is simplicity, it would be much easier to come in and pick out a percentage right out of the sky and that would probably have more bearing on discrimination than what is going on. I am speaking just as a lawyer on the practical aspect, not as an actuary.

Mr. Gibb: I am still not clear, you know, what your complexity is, but maybe—

Mr. Lesser: I would just comment that I think part of the complexity arises from the fact that the percentage has been reduced.

Mr. Gibb: Yes, this may produce problems in terms of how you should react. Do you lower the percentage for those above the wage base or do you raise the percentage for those below? That may be a complex problem.

Mr. Hubbard: Are those the higher-paid executives? Anybody who is making just a little bit more than the Minimum Wage Law suddenly becomes a high-paid executive?

Mr. Gibb: They are not the only ones who are in the plan, Russ, you know that.

Mr. Hubbard: No. All I am saying is that I am not quite sure that Congress, in its wisdom, when it passed the original act, had as its frame of reference in discriminating in favor of higher-paid employees those close to the maximum wage base, or even $6,600.

Chairman Biegel: I told you this was going to get acrimonious. We may have a fight before it is over.

Mr. James F. Pangburn, Mellon National Bank and Trust Company: In the proposed regulations, as I read it, there is very little mention or explanation of profit-sharing application. We now permit, in effect, a 9⅜ per cent of pay contribution on earnings over $4,800 in a fully integrated profit-sharing plan; presumably, the equivalent of the pension's 37½ per cent. Going from 37½ per cent to 30 per cent is an 80 per cent reduction—but reducing the 9⅜ per cent under profit-sharing to 6 per cent is a 64 per cent reduction (80 per cent of 9⅜ per cent would be 7½ per cent). Would you comment upon the reduction rationale in going to 6 per cent? And if you apply a further reduction, applicable to new plans at $7,800—where we, a moment ago, agreed that we are now in the 19 or 20 per cent area in pensions—are we talking about a 4 per cent contribution? And if so, how will it build to the full 6 per cent over the years?

Mr. Gibb: Well, first let me talk just about the 6 per cent and then Dan will talk about the other.

The 6 per cent, as I understand it, comes from two sources. Two things happened. The old percentage was 9⅜ per cent. First there was the reduction that comes with the 37½ per cent to 30 per cent, and the second was a change in the interest assumptions. It is assumed now that an employer contribution to a profit-sharing plan will earn more interest than it was assumed in deriving 9⅜ per cent.

Dan, Is the sliding wage scale applicable to the profit-sharing plans?

Mr. Halperin: There are two parts to it—

Mr. Gibb: I don't know whether you mean that the wage base will build up.

Mr. Halperin: You wouldn't have the same problem in the profit-sharing plans that you have in the excess plans. The contributions of the profit-sharing plans are on a year-by-year basis. You could use $7,800 for a profit-sharing plan right now. You don't have to worry about it. You have the same kind of thing, of course, with a pension plan, which is also year by year, so that the concept of reducing the 6 per cent to some figure—if you want to use $7,800—is not involved.

Chairman Biegel: As I understand it, you can start a new profit-sharing plan at $7,800, giving 6 per cent above. What do you do with existing profit-sharing plans which are integrated at $4,800 and which you want to move up? Can you move up quickly to $7,800 at one stroke and give them 6 per cent?

Mr. Halperin: Under the proposed regulations you could either give 6 per cent at $4,800 or give it at $7,800. If you wanted to move in the middle you would have a problem. This kind of problem is one of the things we have been considering pretty actively over the past few weeks, and I think we would want to hear from people who think that they want to do that in profit-sharing plans and exactly why and how the present rules—or the proposed rules—would interfere with that and what they would like to see done to change it.

Mr. James A. O'Connor, Morgan Guaranty Trust Company of New York: In arriving at the new integration limits through a mathematical approach, I would like to know what the rationale is for disregarding the value of the social security benefit after taxes.

Mr. Gibb: What you are really saying is that you should be able to give, I take it, a pension over the social security wage base that is equal on an after-tax basis to the 30 per cent social security pension on the basis that social security is exempt. All I would answer to you on that is that if you want to apply the nondiscrimination rules on an after-tax basis, logic would say you would also do it in computing what an employee's wages are while he is working, to figure what kind of contribution you can give him.

For instance, if, with a money purchase plan, you are going to give 10 per cent of wages, your theory would say that means 10 per cent of wages after tax, and I think you would find out that the higher-paid people would come out a lot worse if you took that dual approach.

Mr. O'Connor: I think that regardless of your tax bracket, one dollar after income tax is worth more than 100 per cent.

Mr. Halperin: I think the point that Bill is making is that if you look at the social security benefit as a percentage of after-tax pre-retirement income and look at the retiring employee's percentage of after-tax pre-retirement income, you would find that there is discrimination in favor of higher pay, and I don't think that anybody really wants us to carry out the implications of that.

Chairman Biegel: This concludes our symposium. I want to thank all the participants and panelists as well as the audience for making these sessions highly stimulating. I am certain the thoughts and comments expressed here will leave their imprint on the direction any legislation or administrative action will take in this area.

PART FIVE

CURRENT LEGISLATIVE DEVELOPMENTS

CHAPTER XVIII

CURRENT LEGISLATIVE DEVELOPMENTS

LAURENCE N. WOODWORTH
Chief of Staff, Joint Committee on Internal Revenue Taxation

I HAVE been asked to speak on "current legislative developments," presumably with emphasis on aspects which are concerned with pension legislation. If I were to interpret the word "current" narrowly, this would limit my topic to this session of Congress. The generally accepted view is that the current session will last until about a week from tomorrow.

This view of "current" would limit my topic to four or five bills favorably acted upon by the House Ways and Means Committee and to one bill which is before the Senate at the present time. The bill before the Senate has already been debated on the Senate floor, before the Supreme Court nomination came up. It was set aside as a result of that action and it remains so at the present time. It may be taken up again, however, and be subject to further consideration in the Senate this week. This bill is H.R. 2767, the House version of which dealt with the tax treatment of soil and water conservation expenditures. When the bill was reported by the Finance Committee, however, it contained seven additional provisions, and about four more have been added so far in the floor consideration. Three of the provisions that have been added by the Finance Committee or on the floor are concerned with pensions, at least to some extent.

RETROACTIVE APPROVAL OF SINGLE-EMPLOYER PENSION PLANS

One of the amendments to this bill offered in the Finance Committee would treat any plan entered into between union representatives and a single employer as a qualified pension plan from the time contributions were first made under the plan, if the Treasury Department determined that the plan presently is meeting all requirements of law; if no disbursements in past years were made contrary to provisions of law; and if the contributions to such plans were not used in a manner which would jeopardize the interests of the beneficiaries. There already is a provision in existing law which provides in the case of multi-employer plans, where these conditions are met, that the Treasury Department can approve the plan retroactively. This amendment would provide the same treatment for single-employer plans.

Discrimination on The Basis of Sex

Another amendment to H.R. 2767 offered in the Senate Finance Committee is concerned with the issue as to whether qualified pension plans under the tax laws may provide for a "reasonable differentiation" in retirement ages between male and female employees. The question in this case is whether such plans represent violations of laws which prohibit discrimination in employment practices because of age or sex. This problem came up initially as an amendment to a civil rights act when a House amendment was added prohibiting discrimination on the basis of sex. The question presented in the Senate was whether it was proper to permit the retirement of women on an optional basis two or three years before men had the right to retire. The Senate decided this issue in the affirmative, although the issue was closely divided and may well be a point of contention in the House.

Pensions In Community Property States

The third provision in H.R. 2767 concerned with pensions is an amendment added on the floor of the Senate. This amendment deals with a provision in the estate tax law which provides an exemption from estate tax in the case of survivor annuities under qualified employees' pension, stock bonus, or profit-sharing plans to the extent of the amount contributed by the employer. The question presented here is how is an employee's wife's community property interest in his pension rights treated for estate tax purposes when the wife dies first. Under present law this has been held includible in the estate tax base of the wife, because she was not the "employee." The Senate floor amendment—offered by a Senator from a community property state—treats the wife of an employee with respect to this provision of estate tax law the same as the employee himself.

WAYS AND MEANS COMMITTEE BILLS

While the Senate has been considering H.R. 2767, in the House the Ways and Means Committee has been considering a series of bills. These bills are only those which have been cleared by the Treasury Department, and each concerns a separate topic.

One of these bills is directed to a pension matter. It deals with pensions for the self-employed, or what is often called an H.R. 10 type problem. You will recall that where capital is a material income-producing factor in the earning of any income, at one time only 30 per cent of the income could be considered as earned income for purposes of the amount set aside for retirement on a tax-free basis. In 1966, this 30 per cent limitation was eliminated, but only for 1968 and subsequent years. At that time, however, Congress did not amend the feature of the law which involves a three-year averaging provision for contributions to H.R. 10 type plans which take the form of payments on annuity, endowment, or life insurance policies. In these cases, contributions to the retirement plans in excess of the amounts generally permitted are allowed without penalties if these amounts do not exceed what could have been deducted in the prior three years, based on the average income in those years.

Since the 30 per cent limitation applied to income in the years before 1968, for those contributing to retirement plans through these types of premiums, this meant that the effect of the 30 per cent limit was not wholly repealed until 1971. A bill acted upon by the Ways and Means Committee removes this effect by repealing the application of the 30 per cent restriction insofar as the three-year averaging period is concerned in the case of contributions paid in 1968 and subsequent years. This bill has now been passed by the House and will be before the Senate Finance Committee shortly. It could well receive favorable consideration in the Senate before the adjournment date.

Insofar as the current session of Congress is concerned, the bills which I have already described are likely to be the only matters relating to pension legislation which will be considered. In asking me to speak on "current legislation," I assume, however, that you would like to have me discuss matters relating to pension legislation which could come up in the next session of Congress.

As you know, the present Administration is committed by a provision in the Revenue and Expenditure Control Act of 1968 to present comprehensive recommendations on tax reform before December 31 of this year. Whether such a message will actually be sent, I have no way of knowing. Whether it is or not, however, tax reform is likely to be a matter considered by the next Congress.

Of course, it is not possible for me to anticipate all that might be included in such a tax reform program. However, it would seem reasonable that in any such presentation the Administration would include proposals on which it had previously made recommendations, which Congress has not yet had time to act upon.

Tax Treatment of the Elderly

One of the matters on which the Administration previously made recommendations on which no action has as yet been taken, is the tax treatment of the elderly. You may recall that in what became the Social Security Amendments Act of 1967 the Administration also made certain recommendations with respect to changes in the tax treatment of the elderly. The tax committees, however, because of the pressure of work, were not able to consider these proposals at that time.

Three Basic Problems

At least three basic problems have been raised with respect to the present tax treatment of the elderly. The first, and probably the most important, problem is that the present treatment is unduly complicated. The present system can, in fact, be viewed as a "conglomerate." By this I mean that it is a combination of several things. First, it is a credit insofar as retirement income is concerned. Second, it is an exclusion insofar as social security benefit payments are concerned. Third, it also involves the concept of an additional exemption.

Moreover, the retirement credit takes a full page on the income tax return and the space taken is not the fault of the Revenue Service in developing the return form. The difficulty arises, instead, from the complications in the tax law. These, in turn, arise from the fact that the retirement income credit was initially designed to provide the same tax treatment for those who did not receive social security benefit payments as is provided for those who do. This made it necessary in adopting the credit to provide an additional half credit for wives, to condition the allowance of the credit on 10 years' prior work experience, and to limit the availability of the credit in the case of those who continue to work after reaching retirement age. It is these attempts to follow the social security exclusion treatment as closely as possible that gave rise to much of the complexity in the present retirement income credit.

The seriousness of the complexity of this credit is indicated by the fact that we have been informed by representatives of organizations representing retired persons that as many as half of those who are eligible for the retirement income credit do not claim the credit because of its complexity.

Another objection that some raise to the present system is that a retirement income credit is denied persons who for one reason or another have to continue working after reaching age 65. Questions of discrimination have also been raised in the case of those who have no retirement income as such, but only earned income which they derive from employment after age 65.

A third objection raised to the present tax treatment of the elderly is that it provides tax reductions for those in the higher income tax brackets who, despite their age, it is contended have no need for special tax consideration. The retirement income credit, of course, because of the very fact that it is a credit provides a lesser benefit relatively to those in the higher income brackets than to those in the lower brackets. This is not true, however, of the social security exclusion or the extra exemption. The extra exemption, for example, in terms of tax reduction is worth $420 to someone in the 70 per cent bracket, $85 to someone in the 14 per cent bracket, and zero to someone who doesn't pay any income tax.

Recommendations to Meet Problems

It was with the objective of finding answers to the above problems that the Administration made certain recommendations in connection with the Social Security Amendments of 1967. These recommendations would have provided a special deduction in lieu of the present tax exclusion for social security and railroad retirement benefits, in lieu of the retirement income credit and in lieu of the special $600 exemption for those age 65 and over. The exemption proposed by the Administration was $2,300 in the case of a single person and $4,000 in the case of a married couple. Since that time, however, social security benefits have been raised, which concomitantly has increased the present exemption level. Thus, it would seem likely that the $2,300 exemption would have to be raised at least to $2,500 in today's terms and the $4,000 exemption at least to $4,200. In addition, the Administration proposal called for a special deduction of $1,600 for those under age 65 who presently are eligible for the retirement income credit, social security, or railroad retirement benefits.

The full special deduction under the Administration proposal would be available only for those with incomes below some specified level. Under the initial Administration proposal, in the case of single persons, beginning with the income level of $5,600, the exemption available would be reduced one dollar for every dollar of income above that level. For married couples, the point at which this reduction would begin was $11,200. The social security increases, which have occured since this recommendation was initially made, also logically call for raising these levels at which the exemption tapers off to something like $6,500 in the case of a single person and perhaps to $11,500 in the case of married couples.

I should also say that in the case of those receiving social security benefits or railroad retirement benefits the special deduction would never be entirely eliminated. Under the Administration proposal one-third of this deduction, no matter what the income level of the individual or individuals involved, would always be available as a special deduction. The reason is that this amount represents a rough approximation of what the individual contributed toward his own social security benefits and therefore represents the return of capital to him.

Under the proposal modified in the manner I have suggested, with the reduction in the deduction beginning at $6,500 in the case of single persons and $11,500 in the case of married couples, there would be some benefit for single persons, even if they did not receive social security benefits, up to an income level of $9,000, and for married couples up to an income level of $15,700.

The principal complaint which has been made with regard to the proposal has been that it taxes social security benefit payments. This, of course, is true where the social security payment is received in addition to other income. However, the deductions are sufficiently high so that if social security benefits are the only type of income received by the individual or individuals in question, no tax would be payable. Given the $2,500 and $4,200 special deductions and taking into account the personal exemptions of the individual or individuals involved, there would be no tax until an income level of $3,444 is exceeded in the case of a single person and until an income level of $6,000 is exceeded in the case of a married couple.

The impact of this proposal would be to completely eliminate the tax on approximately 600,000 people and to reduce the tax for another 2.6 million people. In large part, these reductions, or this elimination of tax, under the proposal arise from the elimination of the work test and also from the fact that the deduction in many cases is more generous in terms of tax benefit than is the retirement income credit under existing law.

In terms of the retirement income credit, this proposal would result in a tax reduction for anyone now using the maximum income tax credit who is single and has an income of $7,359 or below or who is married and has an income of $12,941 or below.

There is, of course, another side to the picture. Because the special deduction tapers off above specified income levels, there would be those in the upper income brackets who under this proposal would have their tax increased to some extent. This would be true of approximately 1.1 million persons.

OTHER BILLS DEALING WITH PENSION LEGISLATION

Bills have also been introduced in Congress on a number of other aspects of pension legislation. These include bills dealing with portability of pension, reinsurance, discrimination among employees, and full disclosure of information. Some of these bills have been referred to other than the tax committees and therefore probably will not be considered by the committees with which I work. In any event, I believe the prior speakers have dealt with these problems.

Let me mention just a few other possible problem areas, however, which do involve matters that come before the tax committees. One of these problem areas is the method of taxing private annuities. The problem is concerned with the method of spreading the consideration, or capital which the individual has put up, for his own annuity over his life so that he is not taxed on the part of the benefit payments representing a return of this capital. The present rules are in most cases technically correct but also complicated. I believe that changes are needed here, however, to give taxpayers more freedom in making provision for return of their own capital or consideration under simpler rules which they themselves in large part determine.

Another problem, which is important in the case of pension tax treatment, is the issue as to whether professional corporations are or are not recognized as corporations for tax purposes. A number of bills have been introduced making specific provision that professional corporations be recognized as regular corporate entities for tax purposes. Interest in this seems to have died down, however, since the liberalization of H.R. 10 type retirement benefits for self-employed individuals.

The tax treatment of foundations is another matter which is quite likely to be considered in the next Congress, and while this may not directly relate to pension plans, yet often a number of the same requirements are applied to pension plans as are applied to other tax-exempt organizations. Closely related to this are the bills dealing with the so-called Clay Brown type of situation. Both the chairman and the ranking minority members of the Committee on Ways and Means have introduced bills on this topic, and I believe their bills would prohibit tax-exempt pension funds, as well as tax-exempt organizations generally, from acquiring a business through debt financing without payment of any tax on their part.

Questions have also been raised as to the tax treatment of capital gains in the case of pension plans financed through insurance companies. Presently, where you are dealing with taxable organizations, a capital gains tax is payable currently by the insurance company. In the case of mutual funds, however, although a capital gains tax is paid currently, it is treated as if it were paid by the shareholders of the mutual fund. It is entirely possible that similar type treatment might be extended to annuities financed through insurance companies.

A final topic which impinges slightly on the area of pension legislation is the tax treatment of so-called subchapter S corporations. There has been considerable dissatisfaction with the present tax treatment of these corporations because of numerous restrictions presently imposed with respect to the use of the subchapter S provisions. It might be possible to make much more liberal treatment available for these types of corporations if pension plans of these corporations were subject to the H.R. 10 or self-employed plan restrictions. A proposal along this line is in preparation through the efforts of the Treasury Department and American Bar Association.

I hope that in these remarks I have given you some insight into some of the areas of taxation which may arise in the future and which have an impact on pension plans.